Sarah Scherk

My Invisible Kingdom

SCOTT FRIED

TO ROB

YOU ARE MORE
THAN ENOUGH

thank you...

I am grateful to the following people for helping me with this project, as advisors, contributors and editors: Judy Zisholtz, (also for assiduously editing my first book); Eric Murphy; Gila Hadani-Ward; Patti Mittleman; Jessica Beitch; Jessie Star; Danny Zaslavsky; Michele Cohen; Sara Litvak, (for the many hours of transcription); Amy Sacks; Kathy Dodd; Carrie-Lee Teicher; Amie Baker; Laura Herzberg and Kemal Colakel at Notice 51; Susan Kaye; Charlie Wright (for really "getting it"); Joel Mittleman; Jill Manske; Malka Kieffer; Norman Fried; Dierdre Mullane at the Spieler Agency; Jennifer Kelleher; Ponyboy; cousins Nan and Charles; Macair Pilloud; Cheryl Prince and Michaele Taylor, Karen Benezra and Hannah Roth. Props to Adam, the teenager who in two separate emails wrote, "Live" "Because you can." I am ever indebted also to the many teenagers who shared their poetic words and invisible worlds with me and who remain anonymous in this book. Very special thanks to Edward Duran and Tobin Ost. Deepest thanks to my family.

For my father
who in his final days, in sleep
whispered my mother's Hebrew name

Your memory presses against me
like the sun on my back
as I stand before my future

I have loved and I have lost
Now I understand the hearts of others

Published by:

Scott Fried
P.O. Box 112
Old Chelsea Station
New York, NY 10113

ISBN: 0-9649046-1-X
Printed in the United States of America
Library of Congress Catalog Card Number: 2004092744

Book Design by notice51
Author Photo by Michaele Taylor

For information on how to order more copies of this book or on Scott Fried's lectures, please write to the address above, or call (212) 465-2646 or visit www.scottfried.com

table of contents

I am a traveler in limbo, all rusty-eyed and grinning
Like the side-of-the-road wheat I am flirting
with flying away
I can't tell where I'm going, where I'll end up or
who I'll be when I get there

In the cozy dwelling far down the path of dreams
I am holding your hand
I am not perfect
I want to be remembered
I must know...do you feel the same?

— Collected from random teen letters

1 | are we there yet?

No one is ever truly alone, unloved or invisible.

Everyone I meet is waiting for something: the evidence of love's arrival; the emblem of answered prayers; the next bus to anywhere new.

Everyone I see is searching for something: the courage to love undefended; the chance to be put back together again; forgiveness.

Everyone I know is haunted by the memory of something: the sound of a train pulling out of the station; a lover's touch in yesterday's rain; that final embrace.

Everyone I teach is worried about something: the silence in conversations with new friends; being forgotten; emptiness.

Every one of us has a wish we whisper: in the hollow of a lover's shoulder; in the Sabbath wind; in sleep.

Upon the inmost roads, we are wistful and we are wanderers, teenager and adult alike, longing for mercy in the promise of tomorrow. In the words of fifteen year-old Noah, "I'm not sure what it is, but I know it's out there."

When I was a teenager, my favorite book was called *The Adolescent Survival Bible,* with topics ranging from how to deal with rejection to how to buy a used car. I carried that book everywhere I went until the binding cracked. I buried it at the bottom of my knapsack, stashed it on the shelf of my high school locker and held onto it under the covers in the darkness of my bedroom. There was never any one particular chapter or answer that helped me the most. It was the knowledge that there were other teens, secret seekers like myself, with the same questions and that there was someone out there who cared enough to take the time to notice us, to hold our concerns and to love us from behind our shadows. Since then I have always believed that it is not in the answer to a question, but in having the permission to ask it, that we learn. It is in opening up enough to talk, to reveal our oneness, to surrender, that we are healed. For if the questions are part of the itch of life then behind them is an awareness that, in a single moment, we are one with others. In our commitment to growth, the objective is learning to love the questions themselves.

Who are you?

What is the meaning of time for you?

What are you scared of?

What are you excited about?

What's going to be your mark on this life?

What is the personal integrity that your soul has to offer?

Whose arms do you fall into?

Where does your echo go at the end of the day?

Who is waiting up, holding the space and making it safe in the middle of your existential night?

And how comfortable are you answering these questions with the words,

"I don't know?"

Richie was my 73rd friend to die of AIDS. At his funeral, while his companion read the opening page of a diary he left behind, the room fell silent. We eavesdropped upon his discontinued private world. On the first page of that notebook, he wrote of promises and plans for the approaching winter. Richie wrote of beginnings and renewal with a familiar, easy eloquence. He wrote of hope. Then the reader tearfully said, "Maybe I'll publish these one day." Suddenly, I began to consider my own journals and even more importantly, my own existence. Although diagnosed with HIV a few years earlier, I had been rendered a life filled with blessings. Yet I had also lived behind too many unopened doors. In those early years of AIDS, it was only a matter of time before these same friends would gather together again for another funeral. The next one might be mine.

Lacking faith that Richie's companion would ever honor this sudden proclamation, I wondered if any of my friends would truly be able to prove my existence by publishing my diaries or telling my story. And was it really their job to do so? Surely I had numerous notebooks filled with journal entries all my own. But was there a way to memorialize myself while still alive? How could I ensure that I would not become just another statistic of the AIDS epidemic and another candle burning through the night in my mother's kitchen on the anniversary of my death?

I began to talk to teenagers with the hope that, in their collective memory, I would not be forgotten. I volunteered at first in schools, synagogues and summer camps, cultivating a sort of ministry. Sharing aspects of the mistakes I made as a teenager and young adult, I inspired them with the lessons I had learned. I memorized their names, answered their questions and collected their prayers. Having amassed an abundance of memorable experiences, I began to write them down. Gradually, this small project was growing into what would one day become my life's work. I came to realize that there was more to teaching than simply securing a permanent place for myself in the past. I could actually assist in ensuring a teenager's place in the future. Soon, what originated as my rejoinder to Richie's journal had developed into an entire book, *If I Grow Up: Talking With Teens About AIDS, Love and Staying Alive.*

The book celebrates those early events, the teens and their stories. In an attempt to condense the knowledge gleaned from years of lecturing and learning, researched and compiled from hundreds of lectures to thousands of teenagers across the country, it has become a guide and even an anchor for my many students and readers. It includes excerpts from my discussions with those teens and touches on topics of love, abstinence, refusal skills, safer sex, HIV testing, activism and death. Also included are samples of poems written by the teens themselves, examining the possibilities "If I Grow Up." Youngsters need to be educated about the risks of dangerous sexual behavior and having their questions answered is a basic right. Accordingly, the book's goal is to empower each teen to understand his or her unique specialness in the hope that such attention will encourage them to opt for safety and a long life.

Since teenagers live on the Internet, emails started pouring in from all parts of the world. In the beginning most of the letters were about gratitude for being seen and understood. As my travels progressed, the content of the emails intensified. The messages in the subject lines changed from "Thanks for coming to my school" to "Here are my problems... and there are many" and "Searching for answers..." One read, "I could sit here for hours and still not know how to get your attention." Others proclaimed, simply "Please listen!" or "Battling me." The questions plumbed even deeper:

Are there any truths you still want to find before you die?

What do you do when you have all this good stuff in your life and you feel too lucky?

Will there be someone to help me along the way or will I grow up alone?

How can I find a person who sees me in a different way than everyone else does?

Can you tell me how to feel comfortable in my own skin?

If we all feel the same way deep down inside, how come it's so difficult for people to talk to each other about their true feelings?

How can you tell the difference between being in love and being deathly afraid of being alone?

Is God what people make Him out to be?

Can I live up to my expectations?

Are we there yet?

One teen wrote, "I feel as if I have so many questions but I don't even know what those questions are." They were beginning to go beneath the surface of their initial curiosity in me and my HIV infection. With a sustained intensity, they were measuring the depths of their own life circumstances and starting to ask the larger questions, outside of how I told my parents about my sexual orientation and if condoms are 100% effective. Though the emails were about the interior of their individual lives, one collective remained: the need to share their stories. "After listening to you speak so candidly about your life and experiences," wrote one teen, "I could not help but return the favor and write to you, not only as a human being, but as a person with a spirit who has struggled and is still

4

attempting to make sense of this struggle in all of its diversity."

At first, I tried to answer each question or issue directly. My ego, in defense of my desire to solve all the problems in their lives, was trying against all odds, to solve all the problems in their lives. Suddenly, I had become the Post-Gen X Ann Landers. In time however, I discovered that they were all really asking the same questions: Can you see me? Am I getting through to you? Will my life be remembered?

Some letters are short, but raw just the same:

Dear Scott, I wish I could realign the stars so I can change who I am and be something more for others to love.

Others are a quick check-in; the dusting off of flaws; the search for nobility:

Hey Scott, I don't know. Life's normal. I'm just kinda coastin' through. I hope to go visit a couple out-of-state schools in a few weeks. I hope leaving this place will make me feel better. Who knows? I'm just back in my little rut, balancing everything, making lots of mistakes and stumbling through high school. At least now I kinda have friends to help me out with it. I don't know. I'll get over my "skitso" kinda attitude soon. If this keeps up, I have no clue. Alright, stay healthy.

Many letters are long diatribes, the unedited rambling of frightened teens alone in their bedrooms in front of their computer screens. Oftentimes, the screen names acknowledge the agony and injury of emptiness: "behindthesewalls," "lookdeeper" and "cryforpeace." Some teens commune in the staccato language of typos and abbreviations, frequently using a lower case "*i*" when referring to themselves. Ever aware of imperfections, one teen wrote, "Please forgive my mistakes; my fingers are shaking on the keyboard as *i* type this." Many of the letters begin, "You probably don't remember me but *i* feel the need to write to you," and "If the world only knew how *i* really felt inside..." Most of the letters end with, "Sorry this is so long but it helps to have someone to talk to. Even if you never write back, it feels better just knowing that someone is listening." They are written with the hope that someone, even an intimate stranger like myself, can rescue the poetry from the pain and perhaps assist in finding deeper meaning in our ever-changing, but consistently confusing lives.

They are written in despair:

I know that I am alone, as in nobody is listening to me and understanding me. I would love to befriend you, but that would be impossible. We may be able to befriend by emailing back and forth, but could you honestly say that you truly think about ME and not just everyone? I know it's selfish but I want someone to be there for me. What upsets me is the fact that there is no 1.

They are written in supplication:

All I can think about is how to find someone else in the world who will stand up and put into words and accept the emotions and struggles that I fight so hard to keep from suffocating me every day. Someone who can give them a name and lend them a face and a voice, and remind me that maybe I'm not quite so alone as it too often seems.

They are written in longing:

These, my braces (for cerebral palsy) are my soul, my heart and my prison and keep me from finding the perfect love. I want to believe that the perfect love will see more than just these, my braces. But how?

They are written in crisis:

I have pulled out almost all of my eyelashes - my most beautiful feature. My life is not perfect. I need that to reflect on my body.

They offer chilling details about eating disorders and self-perceived negative body images; alcohol and drug abuse; sexual molestation; self-mutilation; shame over homosexual feelings; divorce and interpersonal breakups; and more.

As I sit here writing this, nothing I have anymore is worth living for. I find myself driving aimlessly around town as an escape from being at home. On the outside, I am the same happy person that I always was. I get good grades and I'm popular. But on the inside, I don't like myself. I hate myself and I hate my life. I have stopped eating full meals. I am only eating dinner, the one meal that I eat with my parents.

And some letters are from parents:

If only someone had told me to believe in myself when I was a teen.
If only someone had listened to me in my tentative, scared, reaching out years.
If only I had really believed that my life made a difference to others.
If only I would have believed that I was worthy of love because I am –
my life would have been different.

A fellow educator tells me "teenagers are filled with a torrent of emotions that eventually intoxicate. Since they have not yet developed a full sense of self, all that they feel reflects back to them who they think they are. Kids hurt so much because they are such receptors, sponges." Whatever our age, sometimes we absorb the shocks of life into our inner arsenal of emotions until we are soaked in strife. The hurt has to go somewhere. What happens when we feel unworthy and undeserving of any pardon from our pain? What becomes of us when we are afraid to be caught being ourselves? Where, we must ask, is the outlet for all the untamed angst?

Most of the time it is consigned to the world of our secrets, relegated to the province of the misunderstood. There within the quiet corners of our hearts, we settle in, at home, yet at war, with our internal apparitions. Not many of us prosper from neglect, either self-inflicted or otherwise. In the words of one teen, "I want to steal the sun from the sky so everyone else can feel this darkness." Yet just as any secret has a price, a wound disregarded or unabsorbed by a loving other will eventually contaminate. As the letters attest, this is all too often manifested in destructive behavior. A fourteen year-old girl writes, "My best friend went to jail and I wanted to take revenge on the closest thing to me which is myself, so I had sex with a twenty-four year-old." A seventeen year-old boy from Pennsylvania communicates, "When life gets hard for me, I lose control of myself. I start throwing things. Big things, like furniture. I get so angry, I could actually kill someone." And from an anonymous email, "When I think of death, I want life, but when I think of life, I simply want death."

No matter what the specific issue or commensurate destructive belief system and behavior, one constant remains: when we hurt, we erect, inhabit and illuminate the invisible kingdom.

The invisible kingdom is the refuge to which we withdraw when it seems that no one will ever truly comprehend our feelings. It is the place we enter when we are not permitted to articulate the haunting memories of a time when life fell apart. It is the sovereign bond we make with ourselves when we are attacked by the internal voices that echo, "I was there...when you were picked last for the team....when you waited by the phone for the call that never came...when your parents told you they were getting a divorce and you heard the words, 'We're divorcing you!'"

The invisible kingdom is the shelter in the shadow that is cast when we try to express ourselves and are told, "That's nothing. You think you've got problems? You should hear mine!" It is the secret sanctuary to which we ascend when others put a shelf-life on our grief or distress: "You're not still upset about that, are you?" Or worse, "It will pass. You'll get over it." It is the dominion we claim in order to combat an emerging existential void that beckons us to say, "I am completely alone in the universe."

This book is an entryway into that world. One-part love-letter, one-part guide, it is a collection of some of the correspondence sent to me after the completion of my first book. If that can be seen as the story of my life, then this body of work is the life of my story. Yet it represents only a tiny cross-section of the thousands of letters and emails I have accumulated, letters that return us to the once-upon-a-time when life was filled with unblemished expectation. They are the vanguard of unrepressed truth, leading the way towards a reawakening of self. Originally written as personal testimonials and private appeals, they speak to us all.

In part, I wish to ungenerously unburden myself of these letters and the heartache and hope displayed therein. Alternatively, I wish to invite the reader, both teen and adult alike, to embrace the necessity of eaves-dropping on, bearing witness to, and learning from these secret lives. As one teen boldly expressed, "I am no longer a child and I am not living in a friggin' shadow anymore!"

One of my early heroes, the late professor and motivational speaker Leo Buscaglia, once said, "I'd be so much happier if, instead of writing me, you'd write to each other." *My Invisible Kingdom* was written to help facilitate that very process. For in the shared experience of witnessing how others seek faith in a time of loss and confusion, we can all perhaps begin to under-stand why, as one teenager writes, "God keeps throwing stuff at me."

It is my intention that in viewing each letter, the reader will see and hear an important piece of him or herself. For it is in hearing the hearts of others that we can learn to know our own. If we can have compassion for the teens represented in this book, there is a chance that we can find compassion for ourselves as well. Perhaps then we can begin the process of self-acceptance and ultimately begin to terminate the destructive behavior that often displays our sense of unworthiness.

I have written this book in allegiance to this truth and as a reminder of our connection to one another.

In the pages that follow I try to provide what seems like solutions and advice. The truth is, I am not wiser or stronger than any of my readers. I am not closer to God or more beloved than any of my students. I have written this book because I am a rebel poet, myself a part of the faithful fellowship of people who are waiting to be noticed for their questions. Indeed, I am a student of all those I teach.

In addition to the many letters themselves, interwoven throughout this book are two other distinct voices. In ten chapters I speak directly to the reader and in ten corresponding short stories I reflect upon my experiences teaching teens. Each is indicated by a change in typeface.

Over the years my students have become my teachers, my champions and my bounty. Their willingness to embrace a life of self-examination, resiliency and joy is stitched into the lining of my consciousness and has made me a better man. I have written this book so that they may continue to learn how to cultivate the life they want. In kind, they render me to do the same:

You most certainly may use the letter I wrote to you in your book; it became yours as soon as you took the time to read it. It's the least I could give you for what you have helped me gain. I have only one request: while you share my words to help inspire others, I want you follow them too. Live. Because you can.
– Adam, age 19

The teenagers represented herein, in placing their confidence in me, have opened up a window into their secret lives for others to share. In return, my highest priority has been to respect the private providence of their hearts. To retain their anonymity and protect their privacy, most of the names and revealing characteristics in the following letters and stories have been altered. In a few certain cases, however, at the student's strong request, they remain the same. For example, as instructed by sixteen year-old Pete from Atlanta, "Please put more of me in your second book. I want to be remembered."

It has taken six years to complete this project, originally entitled "My Less Than Perfect Life," because of the difficult nature of the material; it incorporates so much of the pain that is hidden behind each teenager's secret eyes. Yet I have persisted, in part for the teenage boy in London who said, "Please Scott, please keep fighting for us." And for the teenage girl in New York City who wrote, "I'm giving God one week to show me a sign why I shouldn't kill myself." And for the many teens who in their letters and emails ended with the words, "Please write back 'cause I have nowhere else to turn."

Most of the mail I have received has been answered; some has not. With the best of intentions, I have allowed some letters to disappear, unreciprocated, onto the lost landscape of my busy calendar. Thus, I have written this book for those students who have been waiting a long time to hear from me and for any reader who can benefit from visiting these invisible kingdoms.

Here is my reply.

I want ultimate happiness

I want to learn everyday

I want a bed with white pillowcases

I want pure acceptance

I want to live near the ocean

I want to play pool and sink the nine on the break

I want a girlfriend with a red pick-up truck

I want the sun to always shine in my life

— Eight teenagers from Connecticut

I can remember the days when I was fearful of
being in bed at night
I can remember the nights I didn't know if
I would make it through
The loneliness of a phone that stopped ringing
The darkness of a sun that stopped shining
The emptiness of a life that has stopped living
Afraid of the night... of the next day

Afraid of where to go... of no place to go
Afraid of myself

With that realization the healing begins
The conversations, The contemplations

How did I get here?

How do I get back?

Do I want to go back?
Going back only means being here again
So I guess forward is my direction
Yes, I will go forward
The healing will begin

Letters from the
Secret Lives of Teens

The tears will continue
And I will still be afraid

But the fear changes...
I am afraid of being happy
Afraid of being happy on the outside and
confused on the inside
Afraid of reaching the highs for a fear of the lows
Afraid of what my happiness will promise others
My happiness will have to be a promise to myself
A promise to allow the sadness
A promise to not ignore the fears
A promise to know when it is okay to go back
A promise to know when I must go forward...

A promise to heal

    — Deena, age 23

2 | my invisible kingdom

My grandfather was a quiet man whose native tongue was Polish, and I was his American-born youngest grandson who spoke the language of the New World: Long Island. My grandfather's skin carried the faint and faraway odor of antiquity, mixed with a hint of whitefish and pickled herring, which I imagined was the mystical scent of streets in the shtetl back in Eastern Europe. My grandfather had a crooked forefinger that I would watch as it traveled across the page of a prayer book, like a pointer, while I sat beside him, propped up against his shirt sleeve, practicing my Hebrew. Years later I learned that he never understood a word of it; he simply enjoyed listening to the sound of my voice carrying on the tradition of our family. It was his way of letting me know that he saw me, heard me and wanted to be near me. It was our time together, time given to my grandfather and me, in folding chairs in the corner of the backyard under the shade of a willow tree, allowing God to squeeze in between our shoulders.

My father bought me my first baseball glove the year that I turned ten. It was a red "Super Flex Web" lefty's mitt, with wide leather lacing stitched along the outside seam and the letter "S" stamped in gold italic above the pre-formed pocket. Even though my brothers said it meant "Spalding," he convinced me that the "S" magically stood for "Scott." My father's voice was as warm and as resonant as the tuba he played in the basement of our house on evenings in summer. The words of his Sabbath sanctification would vibrate through his fingers and tremble through my skin each Friday night as he placed his hands upon my head to pray:

> *"May the Lord bless you and guard you.*
> *May He turn his countenance upon you and be gracious unto you.*
> *May He show you kindness and grant you peace."*

My father taught me to tango, salsa and fox trot on weekend afternoons, while my mother watched from the kitchen. Smiling down on me he would say, "Every boy should know how to ballroom dance," as he held me in his arms and led me around the living room. It was his way of letting me know that he had confidence in my ability to be a kind and gentle man.

My mother gave birth to me on a Monday morning in late September, the same day that Autumn arrived. She did not know she was carrying twins until the moment I appeared. She called me her "bonus." My mother's hand was warm and strong as it held onto mine when we walked up Oakland Avenue and crossed Peninsula Boulevard, practicing the route on the day before I started first grade. My mother used to tell me of the doll she cared for in her childhood that she dragged down the streets of Flatbush in a shoebox with a long piece of string. As a child, I always cried when I heard that story. I now realize it was her way of letting me know that she loved me long before she ever knew the color of my eyes. In a shoebox filled with dreams, she dragged me through her childhood, over and into the next twenty years. On a morning that changed a season, as it did her life, she finally delivered me into existence and smiled into newborn Autumn eyes.

Once upon a time, I felt witnessed and validated, received and remembered.

But like a small child who loses his footing and unexpectedly falls down a flight of stairs, eventually I learned that the world could be a dangerous place. The older I got, the farther the fall. I remember the boy I was in a toy store, standing in front of a rack of coloring books. I desperately wanted the one with the Partridge Family on the cover, but I was ashamed and embarrassed, afraid of getting derided by my older brother and having to run once again into the arms of my sister for perpetual comfort. Instead, I chose the one called "Where's Huddles?" with three guys in helmets and jerseys running after a football.

I remember the boy I was at six years-old in day camp. I was in a group called "The Cadets" and my counselor's name was Mitch. After our morning snack, one by one we would line up and follow him in single-file formation out onto the playground. I was always first in line. With great effort I would extend my gait, step by step, in order to fit my tiny feet into the depressions his sneakers made in the wet grass. I wanted to be just like

Mitch. I wanted his recognition. I had a need for his affection, a craving for his attention. I wanted to be the "All-Around Camper," the guest of honor in his world, his number one. Yet I knew my feet would never fill his footprints; I was only one of his many adoring campers.

I remember the boy I was on the school yard at recess as the other kids would call me by my last name. It felt as if by removing my first name I had somehow become generic and unspecific. In an instant, I had turned into a brand-name pre-pubescent. I was no longer unique or known.

Once upon a time, I did not feel witnessed and validated, received and remembered.

In my childhood I shared everything with my identical twin brother: birthday cakes, clothing and affection from others. Friends, fantasies, even punishments were all wrapped up and bound into a singular memory. Most people could not tell us apart; in fact, to this day, even I can not distinguish which face is mine in any childhood photograph taken before I was nine or ten. On visits with family friends and distant relatives, I sheepishly shrugged off the constant refrain, "What's your name? Which one are you? Are you the smart one or the actor?" Couldn't I be both? One-part proud of our secret language and the extra attention we were getting, I was also one-part hurt, having to share an identity.

In the darkness of our shared bedroom we lived out an entire childhood of late-night closed-eye conversations. The beds were placed together in an L-shape fashion with our pillows positioned head to head. My mother once worried that we were too close, "breathing on top of each other," fearing we could give one another our germs if either of us got sick. But there was no sense in separating us. When he got punished I felt admonished. When I cried he would crawl in my bed to offer comfort. When we were alone in the dark we were never truly alone.

Then I turned into a teen. After saying goodnight, in the safe haven of my imagination, apart from the bedroom I shared, the house I inhabited and the classrooms in which I daydreamed, I would retreat to the comfort of my unseasoned sexual fantasies. Time after time, no matter how hard I tried to prevent it, invariably on the screen in the movie in my mind appeared someone of the same sex. I was demolished. My fantasy life was the only place I knew where I could be perfectly private and effectively safe as a young teenager. But my fantasies frightened me. Worse, I knew as I lay on my pillow so close to my brother's that the pictures I was seeing in the darkness behind my eyelids were different from those in his head. Self-conscious of the coming apart of our union, I believed I had chosen the darker path. For the first time in my life, I felt truly separate and alone.

Around the same time, one weekend of every month, my father would take me on a drive to Great Neck, so he could get a haircut. As a pre-teen on those coveted rides, I would talk and talk, while looking out the window, secretly wishing he would drive slower. So filled with self-esteem and an early sense of pride, I worried that all the people we passed standing on the sidewalk would never get their chance to meet me. I simply could not wait to be noticed. Now, with adolescence encroaching and my life picking up speed, I looked out the window in silence, hoping my father had not yet learned the language of my newly-formed fledgling fantasies, secret shame and constant confusion. The bewildering disposition of puberty was beginning to take root.

Like every teenage boy between the years of 1976 and '81, I would stare at the poster of Farrah Fawcett in a red, one-piece bathing suit; Charlie's favorite Angel, smiling lasciviously at me, somewhat ironically from the door to my bedroom closet. With a forced optimism, gazing in her direction, I would study her features: white-toothed smile, trademark flip-curl hairstyle, nipples. Waiting in vain for an end to this so-called phase I was going through. An invitation to the club of manhood. An erection.

At camp, I had evolved from a grass-stained, skinned-kneed "Cadet Boy" on the kickball field into a sexually confused "Super Senior," guarding furtive glances in the locker room. I remember once surreptitiously stealing a look at Austin as he changed into his swimsuit. Only three years older and a counselor-in-training, Austin was the object of every Super Senior girl's affection. And mine. So it was with both delight and dread during the end-of-summer camp musical, *Grease,* as I performed my big number, that I looked out onto the crowded gymnasium floor and saw him staring up at me.

"Summer lovin' had me a blast. Summer lovin' happened so fast." The look of him, cross-legged as he sat under the basketball net, head tilted to one side, his handsome gaze on me. Finally, for a moment, only me on Austin's mind. "Tell me more, tell me more, but you don't have to brag..." Austin in the locker room. Austin on the gym floor. Everywhere Austin, listening only to me. "Then we made our true love vow..."

I was confused, yet I had neither the language nor the courage to decisively articulate, "This is my burgeoning sexuality; and if this is what I'm feeling then I must be what they call a homosexual." Resolute in my denial, there was definitely still something inside of me that felt different. While other kids my age seemed to slip into the suit of puberty and move ahead without any seeming awkwardness or shame, I felt like I was standing still. "Summer dreams, ripped at the seams..."

Crush after crush, my proverbial closet was getting crowded. I had begun to live in two worlds of real and imagined pain. Gregarious on the outside, I never had a growth spurt, a face full of zits and a voice that cracked as it deepened. Guarded on the inside however, I was growing faster than my mind could keep up with. I was abounding in blemishes and self-perceived defects that I felt lined my character. And my voice was changing all the time. Every so often while I would try, in my adolescent need, to fine tune the chaos on the inside with the calm on the outside, the two worlds would collide. I longed to be seen, yet I was afraid of being found out. In fairness and in truth, as a high school student, I was well-liked and welcome in any clique. Popular, talented and outgoing, I had great friends, above-average grades, and style. I was happy; I was "in." There were moments, however, and sometimes even within the same day, that I felt terribly alone and misunderstood. Those were the days when teenagers used words like faggot, reject, retard, loser, chump, nerd, dork, pansy, pussy, slut, whore, twinkie, faygella, idiot and wuss to define anyone who was different from the rest of the crowd or to describe something that was perceived as unnatural, aberrant and wrong. But there was an even simpler yet more devastating phrase that seized the power of all these words with one swift strike, one that every teenager today knows:

"That's So Gay!"

To quote one of my sixteen year-old students, "Sticks and stones may break my bones, but words will break my heart." To many, I was a winner. To myself, I was a contradiction. To Butch, my 9th grade bully, I was a "faggot," which definitely meant that I was broken, frail and probably gay.

Butch, whose real name was Lawrence, had a sly, sinister smile, short spiky hair and seemed to always know when I would be rounding the corners of my high school hallways. He never actually touched me, but in calling me names I felt beaten just the same. Looking back I suspect that, while going through his own teenage turmoil, he was angry at the world. Probably worried that he could never live up to his nickname, he took it out on me. I now regard Butch's behavior as a way of polluting his own reflection. He saw something in me that he did not like in himself, so he had to destroy it. Perhaps he felt that in exploiting my frailties he could overcome some of his own. While teaching a group of eleven year-olds in Nottingham, England, I asked them why they thought some people bully:

"Some bullies pick on people because they're jealous. They feel bad and weaker than the people they are putting down and picking on them makes them feel better and stronger!"

"Bullies often pick on people because they're picked on themselves and it is the way they express their anger and pain."

"Bullies usually think it's unfair that they are different and they want someone else to feel different as well. They want to share the loneliness with someone."

"Bullies aren't a select group of people. Everyone bullies someone."

Regardless of the psychology behind Butch's behavior, and the latent wisdom offered in gentle retrospect by those sage eleven year-olds, the simple question remains: Was it obvious to Butch and ultimately to the world that I was uncomfortable in my skin?

As a first semester freshman at George Washington University, on a Sunday morning after a late breakfast, I came back upstairs to my suite in the corner by the elevators. Room #803. Jaggedly torn out of a page from a magazine and taped to my dorm room door was a picture of a naked man wearing only a black G-string, his arms folded across his chest and a cape tied around his neck. Embroidered onto the G-string, in wide silver stitching, was the letter "Z" for "Zorro." Written diagonally across the page, in bold black marker were the words,

"Dear Scott: This Picture Is For You, Because I Love You! You Fag!"

I stood there for a few seconds in total disbelief. With a bowl of dry Captain Crunch breakfast cereal in one hand and my room key in the other, I stood and stared, then looked around to see if anyone was watching. I had three questions. First, who put it there and what did they know about me that I did not want to know myself? Second, who saw it and how many people had already started to spread a rumor through the building, around the campus and back up to Long Island? Third, and most devastating of all, why can't I look away? I could not stop staring. It was the first time I had ever seen a picture of an almost naked man smiling at me, with my name emblazoned on his chest, and written underneath it, the word "Love." I was both stimulated and ashamed at the same time. If I was attracted to what I saw, then I was indeed a "faggot" and my heart was truly ugly. I took the picture down, folded it in half, and half again and carefully placed it deep into the front left pocket of my jeans. At the end of the semester I transferred rooms. At the end of the year I transferred schools.

Five years later, with an undergraduate degree in classical literature from NYU and no real way of earning a living, I followed my dream of becoming an actor. In order to earn my union card, I took a job as the assistant to the assistant stage manager of an off-Broadway musical. My first assignment was to clean out the trap door under the stage so the actors could use it for a one-second bit joke. For fifty dollars a week, among other menial tasks, I worked quietly and steadily in a crawlspace beneath the stage. As I cleared the area of dust-covered props and cobwebbed costumes, I listened longingly to the actors rehearsing above me, wishing I could walk in their footsteps. I sang along with them as they crooned:

> *The life we lead don't last too long*
> *Live for today*
> *That's what they say*

"What's your name?" I heard a voice that pulled me out

of my brooding reverie. Looking down from the ladder I was perched upon, I saw a man in paint-covered overalls holding a hammer, smiling up at me. He seemed to be in his mid-thirties, with a pock-marked face, long straggly hair and a half-grown beard. He scared me. He entranced me. He introduced himself to me under the trap door. "I see you here every day, working all by yourself. You're so quiet. I'm the guy making all the noise above... building the set. What's your name?"

Climbing down from the ladder, I felt visible. Validated. Vanquished of my isolation. Standing next to him, I felt discomfort. Dread. Delivered into folly. I had returned to that familiar state of contradiction. The song above my head continued:

> *Everybody's got a story*
> *And they tell it pretty well*
> *How they had a chance at heaven*
> *How they ended up in hell*

With a mixture of apprehension and delight the following day, after cutting my finger on an exposed nail under the floorboards, I reached out to him for aid. We sat at the top of a staircase, next to the dressing rooms, this alluring stranger and his harvested young find. He gently held my finger in his hands as he applied some ointment to the wound and tenderly wrapped it in a plastic bandage.

"I know your secret, you know."

"What secret?" I asked.

He smiled and said, "Here's my number. Give me a call sometime." I took the scrap of paper he held out in his hand, folded it in half, and half again and carefully placed it deep into the front left pocket of my jeans. At the end of the day I vowed to never call him. At the end of the month I picked up the phone and dialed his number.

He lived in a one-room flat with a makeshift loft bed in the center of the room, a brown couch by the window and a shared bathroom down the hall. He showed off his jeans that were strategically ripped at the crotch and sat down to play some music on his keyboard. He spoke in a fake southern accent and said, "I wrote this song today, partner. What d'ya think?"

I wore a white t-shirt and a pair of jeans proudly ripped at the knees. I stood beneath the loft bed feeling like an insecure actor on an empty stage. I buried my hands deep into my pockets, unsure of what else to do with them. I told him I liked his music.

I lied.

There are three universal yearnings in every young person's heart. First, to be listened to by someone who can see the things inside that others cannot. Second, to be the most important person at the lunch table, the guest of honor in the world, someone's #1. Third and most significantly, to be remembered, which usually comes in the form of a phone call, email or text message. I feared that if I told him what I truly thought of his music, or that I was ambivalent about my feelings for him, or in some way said or did the wrong thing, I would be putting myself at risk of losing all three honors. We all have some fear that if others knew who we truly were, we would lose their love. I had already taken the long forsaken walk to his apartment on Columbus and 70th. I had already ignored the ominous portent of the broken banister at the top of the stairs. I had already trespassed over the truth into a realm of unclarity. I could not endure banishment back into my invisible kingdom.

I returned five or six more times. Each Monday night, as I took the #1 subway uptown to the 72nd Street station, I felt a little more nurtured, yet a little more terrorized. I never told anyone what I was doing or where I was going. Like many young people in therapy, I lied to my therapist. I made up stories to my roommate. I even denied it to myself, actually believing the voices in my head that screamed, "This will be the last time!" Since he did not belong to any of the circles in which I traveled, I was convinced there would be no way for him to intercept the singular path of my life.

I had stepped outside of one closet and right into another.

The very place that at first felt unsafe to reveal my secrets had now become the only place I could feel safe to reveal my secrets. Effectively, in his company, I was somehow captured beneath that trap door and I could hear it over my head, shutting me in.

Giving expression to a seedling of courage one Monday, I said, "I'm not sure I want to do that kind of sex again, tonight. I mean, I want to, but I don't. I mean...

I don't know what I mean."

"Aw. C'mon partner! You know you want it! Otherwise you wouldn't keep coming back!"

What I wanted was to be held. What I wanted was to be loved. What I wanted was to be witnessed and validated, received and remembered. But the only way I knew how to communicate that was with my body. I believed that if I tried hard enough I could make him love me. When he said, "I like your pecs," I heard the words, "I adore you." When he said, "I like your smile," I heard the words, "You're the one." As a child playing tag with my brothers on the lawn, I prevailed in running away from outstretched arms. Yet, in the playground of his beguiling world, I longed to hear the words, "Tag! You're it."

"I can't love you, partner," he once said, brushing off a tangle of sweat-soaked hair stuck to his jaw. "I can teach you about sex with another man. But I can't love you." Looking back, it was probably the only honest thing he ever said, aside from the night I looked up into his face for approval, when he smiled and declared, "I didn't use a condom that time."

Week after week, lying beneath the weight of his body, I actually wanted to hurt. Gradually, while the pain beckoned with an undue intimacy, my feelings of unworthiness intensified. Somewhere in the month of December 1987, I was systematically diminishing. After a certain point in time, beyond the threshold of physical and mental distress, both now familiar and expected, something inside started coming undone. Silently, I would challenge God, "C'mon, make it hurt more... You can do better than that!" Caught in between a conflict of emotions I fluctuated to extremes, until finally, like a fuse box that flips its switch and blows, I snapped.

With each gentle pat of his hand on the back of my head, hope would rise. *He does care for me.* With each emotionally detached and aggressive thrust of his body against mine, despair would descend. *He doesn't care for me.* With each kind whisper, I inhaled a little life. *He loves me.* With each unkind act of neglect, I died a little death. *He loves me not.* The captivity of emotional ambivalence. I marked the marching of time by lying still, holding my breath and abiding. *Any moment now. It won't be long now.* My total submission had become the ultimate act of defiance, stretching my will, waiting to hit a spiritual wall. *Any moment and it will all be over.* Until at last, I would slip beneath the surface of the pain, excavate my inner core and dig my spiritual grave.

In psychological terms it is called dissociation, a benevolent loan from the depths of the psyche enabling the mind to sufficiently detach when it senses the presence of danger. In emotional support groups it is known as co-dependency, an unhealthy willfulness to subjugate one's own needs for another person's in order to protect an underdeveloped and threadbare sense of self. In a young adult's mind, revealed in all its rawness, it is a longing to be made visible and a craving to fill the existential void - a void created by the recognition that adolescence is the archetypical introduction to separation and loss. One of my students once said, "When we are broken long enough and we just want someone's arms to hold us, we think that sex will heal us." Underneath the weight of his body, blood rushed to different places inside me causing my heart rate to quicken and adrenaline to flood my veins. I had mistaken arousal for intense emotion, leftover scraps of acknowledgment for love. I had developed a learned helplessness and could not imagine survival without some abuse. A strange mix of pain and longing had interfered with my judgment and allowed me to feel a need to attach to someone – anyone – to help me overcome my fear of feeling alone, unloved and invisible.

When I was a teenager, I had a favorite song called "The Promise." Doodling into my notebook during boring high school science class I would write the lyrics to the chorus over and over:

> *...and if I never leave your arms*
> *I really will have traveled everywhere*
> *...for my world is there*

Like most teenagers, I was erroneously taught by society that I must dissolve into a relationship. Instead of connecting my life to another's, I thought I could "complete" my life with a partner or mate. Instead of helping to enhance my identity, I expected to find and adopt a new sense of self. I believed that it was the job of someone else, outside myself, to make me into a finished product. In the once upon a time of post-adolescence, I could never have my happily-ever-after until I had a boyfriend. To quote my friend Shawn, "We need to make ourselves whole to find our own soul's voice. It is not in the face of another person." Yet, this is still an issue for many of my students today. In a recent lecture at an Ivy League college, not one sorority sister raised her hand when I asked,

"Who here is comfortable with being single?"

In an effort to annihilate a self-perceived inner ugliness, I had begun the process of self-erasure. Lying in that loft bed, with the words "Hey partner" whispered into my ear, I felt that I had been invited into my alluring stranger's world. It offered me a sense of wholeness. While it may not have been the best world, it was a world in which I felt I belonged. Perhaps he, another lost soul, was just as lonely.

A male student from New Jersey recently wrote me this email after hearing some of my story:

I'm in a situation like that with someone. I don't like him, but I do like him. I am looking for acceptance and comfort with him because I can't find any within. I feel so wrong when I'm with him...well, wrong isn't the best word, because it's not a matter of guilt or a bad conscience. It's a matter of a pleasure that I take because I fear it's the only thing I can have. Lately, I've been finding myself searching for signs (songs on the radio, etc.) that he really likes me. If I have to do that, then something inside me is telling me that he most likely does not. But he says one nice thing to me, and I'm won over. It's amazing what a few kind words can do to someone who's a little insecure.

Another teenager, who calls herself, "**the girl from the stairs**," confirms,

Sometimes I think I have sex to feel like I belong to somebody.
Sometimes I think I have sex because I just want to hang out all

night at a party and know that HE is looking for me.

*Sometimes I think I have sex because I feel so empty inside
and I don't when I'm with a boy. I always thought sex was
supposed to be wonderful. I mean, it's fun and all,
but it's not what I thought it would be.*

After a month of visits to his loft bed, I got sick. I had high fevers and
night sweats, shakes and chills, body and muscle aches. There were sores
at the back of my throat making it difficult to swallow and red
spots all over my torso. My ears were filled with a piercing ringing and my
head pounded with pressure. Unbeknownst to me, I had the Acute Onset
of HIV, the Primary Illness, the Initial Infection, or the Conversion
Sickness. Poignantly, today it has those four names. In 1987, it had none;
back then we knew so little about the disease.

He came to visit. It was the only time he ever set foot in my apartment.
Carrying two brown paper bags filled with groceries, he found his way
around the kitchen and cooked a pot of potato soup. Within minutes, my
apartment was filled with the scent of salt and spice, care and kindness.
"This'll make you feel better," he said, squinting at the flame under the
pot, lowering the boil to a simmer. As the soup cooked he crawled into
bed beside me and even though I felt so sick, I let him have his way with
me one last time.

I remember him, salt-sweated and sunken-eyed, his crooked stare bearing
down. I remember me, the low end of normal, the insignificant other
lying at the intersection of risk and need. When he was done, he rolled
over to the wall and with a glancing touch of his hand against my forearm
said, "You know what partner? Now I can tell you that I love you."

After two weeks, finally able to lift my head off of my pillow, I went to the
Department of Health for a battery of tests: syphilis, gonorrhea, HPV
and a host of other sexually transmitted infections. At the clinic, I was
asked if I had been having unsafe sex. For the first time ever, in the
presence of two strangers, a male doctor and a male nurse, I told the truth.

I met with him later that afternoon at the 2nd Avenue Diner on 29th
Street. The restaurant with the green front awning was empty except for
one waitress and a table of older women lunching in a corner. He chose a

table on the other side of the room, one with a green and white vinyl striped tablecloth with matching fabric on the chairs. We ordered two cups of tea as I told him about my experience at the clinic. Hoping to make him proud I said, "I did exactly what you told me to do. I gave them a fake name and asked for a syphilis test."

He looked away but nodded his head in approval. "Did you ask for the doctor I suggested?"

I halted, wondering how to defend my answer. "No," I finally submitted. "They gave me a number, I waited in a room with everyone else and when they called me in, I held out my arm."

Almost speaking into his cup of tea, he said, "Uh-huh."

"...and then they suggested that I get an HIV test."

He put down his cup and looked through me with a scornful stare. He was silent for a long time. "And did you?" he finally asked.

"Yes," I answered, feeling the perilous oncoming of a sudden storm. "I mean... they said I should and all... so..."

"Did you tell them my name? Did you tell anyone my name?" His delivery was direct; his intention clear. Riding the arc of his rage he asked, "Are you insinuating that I infected you?" The lunch ladies stopped their conversation and looked over at our table.

"Because AIDS is in the water you know!" I knew that it was not. With the hard heels of his hands against the edge of the table, he pushed his chair away from mine as the tea splattered. He stood over me. "If you tell anyone I infected you," he continued, leaning in towards my ear, almost whispering, "I will kill you."

"No." I mumbled. "No... it's not like that... I didn't tell anyone. They suggested that I... and I kind of agreed and all... and the next thing I knew..." My eyes trailed behind his body as he headed for the door. In the next instant, he was gone. I looked over at the ladies in the corner, picked up the wet check and walked over to the cash register. As I reached deep into the front left pocket of my jeans for some money, I realized I could not leave the diner until I had paid for his tea. I knew then that I was infected with HIV and I was already paying the price for my mistake.

I know a teenager in Kansas who was approached and seduced on the Internet by a man in his mid-thirties. Nineteen year-old Danny declined. "I don't want to lose my innocence yet," he explained to me. "I want to experience the emotional learning curve with others who are going through it at the same time. Others my age. Older people lose their innocence because life gets complicated. I want to find someone who hasn't gotten complicated by life and lost that innocence."

Walking out the door of the diner, years before Danny would become my student, I was beginning to learn that same lesson. I crossed the street and stepped inside another diner, this one filled with many people. There, among the noise and movement of a New York City afternoon, I sat down and ordered some lunch. As I lowered my head, a beautiful young woman sitting at the next table saw me crying.

"Can I help you?" she asked.

I wanted to reach out to her and tell her my entire story. I wanted to be held. I wanted to be loved. What I wanted was to be witnessed and validated, received and remembered. I looked into her eyes for less than a second and said, "Thanks. But I'm fine." And I heard the trap door to my invisible kingdom slam shut.

On an unexceptional morning in the early June of my least favorite year, I stood in the office at the Department of Health, waiting to receive my second set of test results. My first round of tests, months earlier, reflected all the sexual activity, both physically and emotionally safe, in which I had engaged before I met my alluring partner. This second set of tests, six months later, reflected the events in the loft bed in that apartment at the top of the stairs. Once again, I felt like an insecure actor on an empty stage, unsure of what to do with my hands. Then I heard the words, "I'm sorry... it's positive."

Time stopped.

The room exploded into emptiness. My eyes saw only the white of absence. Gone, the four cinder-block walls that shut out the smell of fear in the waiting room. *Positive.* Gone, the gray metal desk the test counselor leaned against, manila folder in hand. *Positive.* Gone, the expectation of relief, the involuntary ability to ever again exhale. *Positive.* I tried wrestling the word away from my ears, which were instantly flooded with blood, but I was already immobilized and pinned to my past. Pieces of my childhood broke up into particles and projected themselves onto the now bare canvas of my mind as a series of fugitive moments: my mother's profile...the back of her head...my father's voice...Sunday morning sunlight through a window...the brown dresser in my childhood bedroom...a stuffed animal...my mother's left hand gripping a white rag...my father calling out my name... 'What have you done this time, Scotty? I can't fix this one for you. What have you done?'"

Moments later, with some phone numbers in my hand and a souvenir in my bloodstream, I walked out of the test counselor's office and back into the waiting room. Time had somehow re-started. With the word "positive" repeating over and over in my ears, the noise of the day rushed back in, deadening its echo. I heard a television set blaring reruns of the old game show, "Let's Make a Deal." I heard a song on the radio at the reception desk, Neil Diamond's version of the theme from *Les Misérables:*

> *I had a dream my life would be so different from this hell I'm living*
> *So different now from what it seems*
> *Now life has killed the dream I dreamed*

I heard the vibration of my footsteps descending the empty stairwell. The creak of the front door. The silence of the day that lay open before me.

In grammar school, I loved the sound and feel of mornings in early June. The heavy rattle and easy roll of windows lifting open. The warm weightlessness of air entering the classroom. The dawning of longer days, of light that lingers, of heat that heals. The sound and feel of expectation, announcing the arrival of change. Now standing in the doorway of the Department of Health, I had reached the end of my adolescence. Like shrapnel to my senses, the promise of summer assaulted me. I dug my hands deep into my pockets, turned my face away from the sky and walked past the nameless statue in the center of the courtyard. With a newly carved-out chasm in the landscape of my life, I took a deep breath and crossed the street into my future.

"Today I am not broken," writes a college student, comparing my story to hers:

I choose to believe that everyone has a deep and feeling heart and soul. No matter how much they may try to ignore it or turn it off, it is still there. I believe that if my "advantage-taker" had fully realized how much and to what extent he was hurting me, he might have acted differently. They lash out and hurt because they are reacting to some inner hurt and bitterness of their own that they hope to ease. I feel sorry for them because they do not know a better way to heal themselves. It's not about solving the pain. It's about living with it and surviving it.

It would be many years and countless lessons later that my friend, Cheryl, would lead me by the hand back to the center of that courtyard outside the Department of Health. On a late October evening, there in front of that nameless statue, we would dance.

Today I am not broken. I've been there and tomorrow will be better.

Once, in my travels, I found myself telling my story in front of nine hundred teenagers in a Wisconsin high school auditorium. One student in the crowd shouted out, "Did he know he had AIDS?"

"I found out years later," I answered, "through a strange series of coincidences, that yes, he did know he was infected with the virus while we were having sex." I recounted for her and the rest of the students the dream I once had where I finally found the courage to ask him, "Why? Why would you knowingly infect me? Why did you do it?" Before he could answer, I woke up and remembered he had already been dead for three or four years.

"Anyway," I shrugged, speaking slowly into the microphone, "I know what he would tell me. He would look at me with that smirk of his and say, 'Because, partner...because...you...let...me.'"

The most dangerous sexually transmitted infection (STI) is not HIV/AIDS. It is the hollow feeling that the heart forbears the second you awaken to realize that you let someone else borrow your body for a joyride, to explore and exploit. The most common STI is a self-inflicted broken heart. I am partly responsible for my HIV infection. I am obliged to protect my body and my emotional life.

I am no victim.

In my travels I have learned that it is always the student in the back of the auditorium, sitting on the left side, second or third row from the doorway, that offers up my finest challenge by asking the hardest question of the day. This time it was Brad. "The guy that infected you...if he were here right now...what would you say to him?" It is always that student in the back of the auditorium that asks the question I have never been asked. I started by thinking out loud.

"Well," I began, "let me say this. I never ever mention his name, but I will today. His name was Paul. But he called himself Racey. He made it up himself. He said it made him sound like some sort of underground superstar." And under my breath, but still into the microphone, looking down at the stage and thinking of my answer, I whispered, "What a stupid name."

A crash of laughter. An absolute shattering of joyful noise hit my ears. I looked up and realized I was speechless. Stunned. Unworded. "You're laughing!" I exclaimed. "At his name! At me making fun of his name!" And in an instant, the many years of fear and shame seemed almost slightly comical. They were helping me laugh at myself. My students were assisting me to loosen myself from the weight of his memory that I had been pinned under for so long.

"I never say his name out loud," I explained, this time starting to work the crowd, seeking more release from them, "...because I'm afraid I'm gonna invoke his spirit and his ghost will be flying over me, hovering around the room."

Another crash of laughter, this time louder than before. In front of a room full of teenagers I was daring to feel, for the first time, the tiniest bit of glee. I was standing before a fresh brigade of bodyguards, an auditorium of brothers and sisters, witnesses to this release. They had startlingly become protectors of my future and believers in my ability to be more than my mistakes. Standing in my vulnerability, I was poised to prove that I can exhume his name and even his memory from the spiritual grave I had been buried in, no longer needing to solemnly stand sentinel over my past.

I looked over in Brad's direction in the dark of the theater, at the back by the doorway and imagined his face. What did he look like? Was he laughing, too? I collected the words about to leave my lips in answer to his question.

"Brad, if he were here right now, I'd say, 'Guess what? You didn't get me. You will never get me. Because I am still alive. And no longer trapped. In spite of it all, I love my life!'"

There were twenty-four panels from the Names Project AIDS Memorial Quilt hanging from the fly space behind me. And on the floor of the stage at my feet, a huge white sheet was filled with expressions and written sentiments from the teens to people they had lost or had never even met. Written in purple marker and signed "Andrea, '98" were the words: "We are all just trying to make it."

I wouldn't appreciate life unless I had my past mistakes behind me.
Do you think we need to make these mistakes? It seems to me that without learning for ourselves, we won't appreciate it when the right thing comes along. Do you think we're more connected with ourselves when we've been lost and then found?
– Meg, age 20

As a boy in hebrew school, I used to love the characters in the Bible who lost their way in life only to find themselves again - the early figures who struggled to earn their grace, like Jacob. Along his painful journey, midway through the story of his life, he is beaten by an angel while he sleeps. They wrestle till dawn until Jacob is bruised and broken; then the angel begs to be turned loose. But Jacobs insists, "I will not let you go until you bless me." He exacts a blessing from his assailant. He demands sanctification from a curse in the middle of his existential night, before the dawning of a new day. "What is your name?" the angel asks. "Tell me who you are that I might bless you." Upon Jacob's reply, the angel blesses him, as is customary in the Bible, according to Jacob's capacity and ability, by giving him a new name. "You shall be called Israel, for you have wrestled with beings human and Divine and have prevailed." Only after he struggled was the blessing given. In fact, the struggle itself became the blessing. This transformation affects his future and the future of generations to come.

Everyone wrestles with Jacob's angel at some point in their life.

Once I heard someone say, "You learn a lot about life when your dreams don't come true, when nothing works out the way you planned." After surrendering to life's demanding circumstances and yielding to a higher plan, I have learned it is in the permission to tell my story that I am blessed. It is in the rare privilege to accept the struggle and proclaim my aliveness that I am refashioned. It is in the answer to the question, "Who are you?" that I am renamed.

I am Leon's youngest grandson, as I wrestle with Jacob's angel, lifted off the page of a prayer book beneath my grandfather's crooked forefinger. I am my father's worth, as I dance through adulthood under the canopy of his paternal pride.

I am my mother's bonus.

Each time I visit and reveal my invisible kingdom, I am once again witnessed and validated, received and remembered.

Leapin' Lindsay

I am a world away at summer camp. Standing on the edge of a circle, among seven hundred hungry campers welcoming the weekend, I am readying my heart to absorb the charge that stirs this place.

Here, amidst the din of noise at the flagpole, is an endless supply of catalysts for each of my senses: distant echoes of adolescent screams after a clap of thunder through the trees; the undertow of mud pulling my sandals towards a deeper and softer ground; the smell of Friday rain; and teenagers everywhere, both starving for and full of worlds just beginning.

Teenagers take kindness very seriously. I return to this camp each summer and, though they have grown, they still hold the memory of once being generously loved and offer it in return, quickly and selflessly. "Hey Scott. I remember you. Sometimes when I'm lonely, I sing that song you sang to us last summer."

And suddenly, the lake feels familiar. The color of light under the leaves on the trees seems just right and I have a sense of belonging again. Of connectedness. Of home. And I remember: Jared is the kid who picks his mosquito bites until they form scabs up and down his legs. Abe is the counselor who writes love poems about a girl back home he's never even kissed.

Girl. Yet like a knife to one crushed in shadow of winter storm. Then I lay beside you. Gorgeous. Frantic. Delicate. I need. I want. I watch you walk away.

Finally, Lindsay is the cognitively impaired teen who won the "Leapin' Lindsay Award" for learning how to dive into the swimming pool. She leads me to the tennis courts one night to show me the stars.

"Tell me about the full moon, Lindsay. What do you see?"

"It fills my heart with light," she sings. Exultant and proud, she walks away, turns around and adds,

When you look back on these days, remember to remember me.

I am passing people along the pebbled path in the black of night. I am waving in the dark to someone I've met in an earlier summer, as if we've passed this road a hundred times before. So familiar. No longer precious or rare or even too beloved. Just the everyday abundance in the everyday life of a teenager. ♔

Dear Scott,

I don't want to wait any longer for someone to ask me, "Who are you?"

I am a white woman in college majoring in Critical Gender Studies and Psychology. I dance (always have, always will). I love working with children and I am the oldest of four kids. I didn't have the easiest childhood, but I've made it through and it's a part of me. I am not claiming the title of victim, nor do I consider myself a survivor. I am simply living out my life - my blessed, sacred, difficult and wonderfully contradictory life - day by day.

I am constantly in a process of de-constructing my identity in order to reconstruct it once again. I challenge myself to have a foundation in my values, beliefs and sense of self. My spirit is the light that illumines my life and guides me to incredible places and people. It is the people who shower me with love that keep me visible. I have friends spread out all over the world on every inhabited continent. I have danced on stages across the globe. With each lover, each journey, each adventure, each performance, I learn so much. I discover a new place, a new emotion, a new me.

My life is a contradiction. I have broken some hearts and I have had my own crushed a few times as well. I pride myself on being a mature young adult, but I go to summer camp every year to be a kid again for a few months. I'm a vegetarian but I wear leather boots. I am a feminist struggling with body image issues. I am an independent and strong individual, but I have a weakness for love and loneliness.

I am attracted to both men and women (bisexuality is probably my favorite contradiction). To many people, I am someone to come to for advice, comfort, understanding and direction. But I am also lost in this world and seek guidance of my own.

My life is a beautiful, wonderful, frustrating contradiction, but I stay true to it and true to myself. And I have begun to enjoy living on both ends and everywhere in the middle of the spectrum.

— Jessica, age 20

Did you used to have all the answers,
or did you just think you did?
I am realizing more and more how life is poetry.
We exist in a rhythm, a rhyme that we create
every day of our existence. Sometimes it makes sense.
Most of the time it's just a collection of sounds and
instructions that somehow we must sort through
and find meaning out of. That is the fun part,
I guess. I am so glad that I am discovering this
side of myself.

— Rebecca, age 18

3 | contradiction

There's a teenager in Yehud, a city outside Tel Aviv, who sports a buzz cut and has a fantastic scar in the middle of his forehead where his hairline begins. He came up to me after a class I was teaching and appealed to me in earnest. "I don't believe in God. And I really want to believe that I am holy. But if I don't believe that God created me and that He exists, then I can't be holy. Can I?"

"Yuval," I stated, "if we can find an answer that you will be content with, then we will have figured everything out, right?" He agreed and was listening intently for my response. "My friend, Eric, does not believe in God," I started. "But he tells me when he is on an airplane and the pilot instructs everyone to fasten their seat belts he hears himself saying, 'Dear God, please get me through this.'"

"I live a life of contradiction," Eric explains. "And that has to be okay with me. I don't make that much sense all the time. I say one thing and then I do another. I believe in something and then it is challenged. The most important thing of all is that it is okay with me that I don't make that much sense."

Yuval picked up his yellow knapsack and tossed it over his shoulder as he listened to me speak. "Let's work on your word 'Holy,'" I continued. I thought of other words like Good or Precious, Rare and Beloved. Yet, standing in front of this teen, all I could utter was the word Grapple. "If you can't believe in God," I started, "then can you at least believe in your aches? Believe in your grappling and in your longing for connection. Believe that in wrestling with this paradox you are not alone. Can that be your religion for now?"

He nodded as he clasped both hands around the straps of his yellow knapsack, now pressing into his chest. "I'll try," was all he would say. "I'll try," and then he walked away.

When I was a teen, I did not know how to accept my sexual confusion, my height and my popularity. I hated myself on bad hair days and loved myself if someone laughed at my jokes. I was the last pick for every team in gym class but the captain of every team at camp. I would constantly say to myself: "I have to know who I am and I have to know right now. I've got to make up my mind. Everyone else seems like they have it all together. And I don't." I lived inside the lyrics of a song written by a friend, "You have walked with princes in the city while I have pulled my wagon in a circle." I wanted the world to see all that I was becoming. Yet I feared the world would see all that I was becoming. In this delightful, imperiled state of adolescence I could not seem to accept the contradictions of growing up.

Somewhere in the process of becoming a teenager, I began leading a double life. I created a shell around myself and although it conforms to what I feel people expect of me, it's incredibly shaky. Inside, I feel like I'm going to burst. What if others find out that sometimes I don't know who I am? What if they can't accept and love the real me? I'm a walking, breathing conflict. I desperately want to be whole, just "me," but it's troubling because I'm not there yet. I need to find out who I am but I'm afraid of the journey and what I might find.
– Jo, age 17

Have mercy on yourself, tremendous mercy. You have opened up to a brand new page at the beginning of the book of your life. You are normal in your hypocrisy, if it be so called. You are on the right track. You are fine. Allow your character to fluctuate and your mind to change. In the center of all the animation, it's still you. Confidence can be a fragile thing, but it exists in you. The side effects of growing up can be tempestuous. You are not crazy. You are just really, really alive. You are beautiful through it all. See that. Be who you are today, and if that changes tomorrow, then be that, too.

Ellie was a friend from college who waited to have sexual intercourse way past her twenties. Finally, at the age of thirty-four she lost her virginity. On the following morning, while working at a record store in the city, she had to wear a t-shirt advertising the grand opening. For thirty-four years she lived as a virgin. The next day she walked through the world with the words "Virgin Records" across her chest. "I live a life of contradiction," she laughed. "As soon as I say to myself, 'I'm not that!' the universe plays jokes with my conviction and challenges me to laugh at myself."

Realize that you are human. You do not have to do this thing called "life" with all that much style. Or shtick. Or finesse. Just show up for it. This is the goal: to show up for your life with a bit of curiosity and laughter, whether or not you are full of grace.

Growing up is all about changing your mind.

The acceptance of that fact is grace itself. You will get thrown off and continue to occasionally act in opposition to yourself. You may find yourself living in extremes in order to work your way toward balance again. That has to be okay. You are trying to figure out who you are. In time you will learn that while your issues may not altogether disappear, they become clearer. And while still making mistakes, you will have a different relationship to the mistakes.

In the words of one teen, "It takes a very strong person to be able to wake up each morning, open the window and smile at the world." Live deeply and keep showing up for life. That makes you a hero.

These internal conflicts within, these contradictions and paradoxes are just a step in a direction. Not the right or wrong direction, just the boundless direction of clarity. Who I am isn't some terse nine-minute diatribe. I am my past and my future. Most of all, I am my "during." The way I see it, externally all I need is a good cup of coffee, some fresh bread and great company. Internally, I need kaleidoscope eyes that see the world, a heart that sees the soul and a surplus of love and such pouring out from within. For even though there is lightning in the sky, I will learn to fly.
– Naomi, age 18

I had a friend whose Hebrew name translated to English means "precious goods: the rarest silver, the finest gold." When I told him this definition he said, "I think I should change my name." We all feel that way sometimes; there is a little bit of that feeling in all of us. There are times in our lives when we think of ourselves as less and there are times when we think of ourselves as more. Sometimes it happens simultaneously. One teen says,

"A couple more years and they'll have to repaint me."

Yet, there is an alchemy in the awareness and recognition of our contradictions. It is in blending our emotions and allowing our confusion that we are transformed into the rarest and the finest stuff, precious goods. Ari from DC says, "As the big top crumbles to the ground, I learn to walk the high wire."

Renee was a student in Michigan who asked, "Isn't it kind of funny, in a sad sort of way, when the thing that can kill you actually gives you life?" Sitting somewhere in a sea of students, she tearfully appealed to me for an answer. "How can I get that gift without actually getting infected with HIV myself? Why do we have to hurt to realize how important life is?

I don't want to have a crisis to understand life."

"You have many names," I told her. "You are both 'survivor' and 'surrenderer.' Being able to sit with the incongruity of the question measures your magnificence; life will lend its lessons in good time." Days filled with confusion do not make you less connected to the rest of us. In fact, the searching is what keeps you to the world. You still belong.

I always thought I would have one single identity through my interactions with the world. Me, Enid. But we live in a world of intersections. The overlap of identities. Combinations. Once in a folklore class we were asked to name some folklore groups we belonged to. That's when I realized that I am the sum total of the stories I've got. They tell a story more complex than any single grouping of identities ever could.
– Enid, age 19

Remember these few principles:

The "I don't know-ness" of life is utterly crucial.
Revere the confusion. Honor your contradictions.
Promise yourself that you will make mistakes.
Then promise to give yourself a break every time you
keep this promise.

Always remember that two steps forward and one step back
is still one step forward.
There is sanctity in awkwardness.
There is beauty in disarray.
There is a healing calm in the eye of every storm.

And finally, keep believing in your right not to do this thing called "growing up" with all that much elegance.

Just keep breathing.

$Zach$ with an 'H'

A few summers ago, I was teaching in a camp in West Virginia. After talking to the older teens about AIDS, sex and the challenges of growing up in the world today, I was asked by one of the counselors in the staff lounge if I would meet with the younger campers between the ages of eleven and twelve. They heard that I was "really cool" and wanted me to talk to them about HIV/AIDS. I had some initial resistance because of their age, but with the counselor's persistence I acquiesced.

"There's just one thing to remember," she added timidly. "They get a little unruly at times and one of them might try to say something to throw you off. So be ready. I just thought you should know." Suddenly loving this challenge, I said, "Bring them on!"

There I sat, encircled by two dozen pre-teens talking about risk, refusal skills and how to recognize the signs of emotional danger. The hour flew by and still none of the campers had disrupted the peaceful flow of the session. But five minutes before closing, a sandy-haired, freckle-faced boy raised his hand and with his head cocked slightly to one side announced, "...um, I have something I've got to say."

"OK," I replied. "Tell us what's on your mind."

"My name is Zach," he said. "Zach with an 'h,' not with a 'k.' Don't forget that. I wanted to tell you," he continued, "that I learned the meaning of life this summer, here at camp in West Virginia. And I'd like to share it with you so you can share it with the other teenagers that you meet."

I sat back and smiled. Then I remembered the magnets I had seen on the refrigerator in the staff lounge, strategically lined up in order to create the phrase: *Teach Me To Love Life.* I listened as Zach told us his story.

"Well you see, it was late at night in my cabin and I was in my bunk, Bunk 24. It was after 'lights out,' past curfew, and I was lying there in the top bunk bed. I was supposed to be asleep, but instead I was whispering in the dark to Matt. 'Whenever I can't sleep,' I told him, 'I talk to God. And I ask God why He made me different from everybody else. Why couldn't He make me perfect, like the rest of the people in the world?'" Zach continued. "I told Matt that I was born with one eye that is blind. All my life I have only had one eye that can see. And when I'm all alone at night, I start to wonder why I'm not like my other friends who have two eyes that work. Why am I different? Why am I different?"

Matt had an answer for his friend. And as I listened to Zach share his story, I pictured the two boys in their bunk beds lying in the dark, secretly mapping out the journey upon their innermost roads.

"That's so funny," Matt answered. "Funny, in a sad sort of way, because I do the same thing too. When I can't sleep, I ask God the same questions, only for a different reason. Y'see, my father died when I was eight," he whispered, "and I miss him. And when I look at my friends and see that they have both their parents, I want to know why God picked on me to be different. Why me?"

Suddenly, when both boys thought that no one else was awake in the dark of the cabin, they heard another voice. "That's funny, because I do the same exact thing." This camper shared about his older brother who is mentally retarded. "I feel like he is my younger brother and it bothers me. Sometimes I have to look out for him and handle his problems. My friends make fun of him and they even make fun of me and I just wish that my life was like everybody else's."

Another camper spoke up, and still another after him. Before long, all of Bunk 24 was awake in the dark sharing their secret worlds. They were talking to each other about their innermost needs and their unrevealed longings. They were discovering the road to their invisible kingdoms.

Then Zach told me the meaning of life as he had assembled it in his mind that late summer night in his bunk in West Virginia. "I learned that there is no such thing as a perfect life and that everybody has something that happens to them." I made him repeat his words, so I could remember them correctly. This time, he added, "Everybody has something that they have to learn to live with."

Yet, the very thing that made him feel different and separate from everyone else was in fact the one thing that connected him to the rest of his bunkmates. In his reckoning with and offering up aspects of his internal hideout, Zach had carefully willed himself to the wisdom of the others. In the quiet pause that comes from recognition, the boys of Bunk 24 were able to bear the impress that Zach's sense of aloneness had created. And from this witness state he was ready to begin the process of accepting his situation.

Finally finding peace, he was able to fall asleep.

Dear Scott,

I am scared. I am scared of showing my emotions. I am scared of appearing vulnerable. I am scared that admitting vulnerability is inevitable. I am scared of losing control of this facade I've created. I am scared of being rejected. I am scared... terrified... of being alone.

You'd think I have it all pulled together. I have an amazing family. I am a great athlete. I have friends, good grades. People like me. I am happy with my body and my looks. I am involved in activities. You'd think I have it all pulled together. But I don't. I never will. "Having it all pulled together," means perfection and no one can have perfection. I feel like no one ever looks at me and sees me. It is so hard for me to write that because my life is wonderful, perfect from society's standards. But it's not. It can't be. It's got to be okay for things to become chaotic, for emotions to flow, for despair to appear and disappear, to have doubts and fears. It's got to be okay.

Three nights ago, I lay in my bed as my boyfriend slept next to me and I felt completely invisible. I felt so desperately lonely. And I don't even know why. I didn't know what to do. I felt pathetic and ashamed because I had no concrete reason for my emotions. But I believe that it is okay to be alive with my emotions.

I walked across campus tonight and I cried. I cried for loneliness in others and in myself. I cried because it feels so good to value my life and my mistakes. I cried because I just want someone to see me and care what I'm about. I want someone to say, "I get you" and for his/her statement to be true. And I fear that I won't ever find the person who can do that for me. I cried. And the tears ran down my cheeks and my face got cold... really cold. But I didn't wipe away my tears because they were real, and things that are real are rare. Sometimes, no matter how uncomfortable reality is, you want to cling to it, to try to make it your own. I find myself absorbed in so much that is false and I can't get away from it. I lie to myself all the time and I don't realize I'm doing it. When I cry, I know I'm being real.

I want to tell these secrets to the people I'm close with in my life. I want to tell my best friend, my mother, my boyfriend. How can I get people to listen to me? It often seems that they don't care to know. They never ask. Though, I never ask them either and I want to know about their secrets. I think we are all so afraid of letting others see our souls, our core. Sometimes it feels so messy and chaotic and this is unsettling. We want perfection. How do we escape that want? We can't have it, but we continue to strive for it.

I am reminded tonight that life is so unbelievably wonderfully special. I am reminded tonight that honesty and realness are refreshing. I am reminded tonight that, in my accountability, I am not alone.

— Janessa, age 18

Dear Scott,

Wuz up? How are you?
Me... I'm just doing my time,
not letting my time do me.
My name is LeRoy and I'm a former gang
member. Right now, I'm a detainee at this Juvenile
Detention Center. When I get out, I will live with my
mother and little brother. My father is in lockup as well,
waiting to get sentenced, looking at ten to forty years in
Federal Prison. I would say life is not fair, that's why
I get high until I die, but you know what? I am tired
of living like this, in the same footsteps of my father,
doing drugs and doing wrong to other people.
Even though I have done wrong in my life, that do not
make me a wrong person. I ask God for His forgiveness
every day and for Him to give me the willpower to keep
going. I guess everybody has a battle in life. Mine is my
addiction to drugs which one day will probably lead me
to an early grave if I don't cure myself and get some help.
From a young man facing his battles I say, "Keep it real
with yourself and hold your head up — cause
life goes on if you want it to."
            — LeRoy, age 16

4 | accountability

TJ followed me out to the field to tell me his story. "All my life," he said, "I swore I'd never do drugs. When I was growing up that was a promise I made to myself. That's the line I said I'd never cross. I might get drunk once or twice," he added, digging a small hole in the dirt with his sneaker, "but I'll never do drugs." Then one day, everything changed.

"In 7th grade I tried pot because I thought it would make me feel better. But it only depressed me. There I was, standing on the line I said I'd never cross. So in 8th grade, I tried cocaine. What the hell? I was becoming the person I said I'd never be. In 9th grade, I moved up to GHB, dust and acid. Once I hid some acid pills in my sock and they absorbed into my bloodstream. I was tripping for four days." He leaned his back against a tree and looked away. "Since I've broken my own rule, there's nothing to hold me back."

"I have a parole officer." he added.

"I need a parole officer."

Everyday, we renegotiate the contracts we make with ourselves. We hit the snooze button on our alarm clocks and promise to get up after an extra five minutes of sleep. We go off our diets and promise to begin anew tomorrow. We cancel plans with friends and promise to make it up to them at a later time. Somehow, we get through. But when it comes to certain other promises, we don't allow ourselves to renegotiate as easily. Instead, we answer the call of the craving and hope that consequence will remain a voice unheard. We become the people we said we wouldn't be, characters at the crossroads giving up all hope of restoration. We self-destruct. Yet if we never learn to renegotiate our contracts or attend to the outcome of our behavior, how are we ever going to learn from our mistakes?

Becoming accountable means answering to yourself in the presence of another. It's busting yourself, tattling on yourself, telling your whole truth. It's trusting the process of disclosure enough to blow the whistle on yourself, listening to your life as you speak, becoming mindful of your thoughts and actions. It's being able to say, "This is the loss I have suffered. This is what I have done with it. This is how I cope. And I want you to listen. I want you to see it. I want a witness."

Becoming accountable means simultaneously witnessing yourself while somebody else witnesses you with unconditional acceptance. It means hearing yourself testify with immunity from shame and any externally or internally imposed constraints. It means revealing to yourself, without any fear of judgment, all that is hidden in the hideouts of your heart. Becoming accountable is the courageous act of placing yourself in the presence of someone who will stand beside you and say,

"Walk with me. Tell me. Let me hear your story."

As directed by one teenager, "It seems to me that when I tell people I am going to do something I am more inclined to do it than just by telling myself."

I met Jonathan when he was thirteen years-old. Once my self-appointed little brother, now a twenty-one year-old young man, he wrote me an email disclosing some of his internal controversy:

*I am in one of those moods where I need to talk to someone and it seems like no one wants to listen, or they don't have the time. I need to get this off my chest. It feels like I am all alone out here. It's like no one I know feels the same way. It's kind of like I am too grown up to talk to my friends about it and no adult wants to talk to me because I am a kid. It just feels like I have nowhere else to go. Everyone says, "You're gonna be great one day. You have so much potential." No one says, "You ARE great." I wish I could call fear "excitement," even though it feels like fear but I am so afraid that I am going to grow up and fail in life and everyone around me will be disappointed. And then again, I'm afraid I'm gonna succeed. I want someone to love me for who I am but I have no idea who I am. Really am. I know who I want people to think I am but I don't think that is really me. I don't know what to do with my life yet. I don't know what I want to be when I grow up. I don't know where I'm going, but I know I'm on the ramp to somewhere. And I think that before I can figure out all the rest of that stuff I need to find **me**. I just need someone to listen.*

Sometimes we don't want the world to see that we are doing the best we can, for fear that they will judge, what Jonathan so aptly describes, "the shit-storm that I call my life." But at the same time, we want to find someone who can compassionately see that we are doing the best we can, even if our personal best is not up to our own self-imposed high standards.

Seek out someone with whom to share your story; but seek with discretion. This is not the "I need help" talk. This is not the "Can you give me some advice?" talk. This is the "Can I get a witness, because I need to hear my thoughts and feelings" talk.

My friend Shawn tells me, "When you can say, 'I am imperfect yet people still love me,' then you will know a new kind of intimacy. It's those small yet beautiful moments with people when there's nothing else but clarity and contact that sustain you." Walk side by side with someone - not online, on the phone or in a text message conversation. Sit face to face with someone - not at a crowded party, at the dinner table or in a note that is passed in class, from hand to hand. Look eye to eye with someone as you talk about yourself. Solemnly declare, "Okay, here I am," and then tell your story.

If you are the person chosen to listen, after the share is over,

here are four helpful responses:

First, "I heard you and this is what I heard you say." Then, with heart-felt concern, repeat back to your friend some of the things that were said so he or she will know you were listening. Try not to offer your opinion of what was said or your advice on what you heard. This is not about your judgment, just your compassion. No solutions, changes or quick fixes. No stealing of anyone's confession. No competition with your own story. Just listen, then say, "I heard you and this is what I heard."

Second, "Thank you for believing that I am a trustworthy person and for sharing your secrets with me." Recognize that avowing the truth in another person affirms your own esteem and worth. For the best way to be understood by others is to try to understand them. They will cherish your secret life in return.

Third, "I love you more now than I did before because I know who it is I love. Because I see you. I get you."

When I close my eyes I see us laughing there
Trying to read the map to figure out what to do
Road signs and stop lights don't mean all that much
We need U-turns sometimes

You let me lead to find out where we were
You tried to trust me and found I was safe
You let me be who I wanted to be
All those years ago

If you need to go back just remember me
Just remember what we said of everything
Try hard to listen
Can you hear us singing?
Friends last forever when travels of the road unwind
– A sorority of girls from Western Pennsylvania

Finally, and very importantly, if a friend is in real danger, or if you think that is where a friend is headed, turn to an adult figure in whom you trust, even if they swear you to secrecy. Are you friend enough to risk losing someone in order to help?

To be witnessed is to be made steady. It is the act of borrowing comfort. It is one of the key ingredients to establishing a healthy sense of self. For our existence to be validated, sometimes we need to know that others see us. They can substantiate for us that we exist in their hearts and their minds. They can help us to say, "I exist because I exist, whether or not I exist in you. But I feel and believe and know that I exist even more, because you acknowledge that which I reflect out into the world." Development of a healthy sense of self relies upon many things, but especially an ability to be recognized and lovingly acknowledged by others.

Dustin is a student who taught me a valuable lesson one afternoon. While acting as a big brother and giving me basketball pointers, he showed me that it is not enough to simply say "I see you." To win the game, "you must take the time to show others that they are important to the team. You must make a connection. You must pass the ball to them."

Yochai, a teenager in Denver, wrote this poem for his father:

Dad, I love you. Why did you have to go?
My life is empty without you. My life is for you.
Every day that goes by I wish you were here.
Every day that goes by I try to make you proud.

Dad, I love you. Why did you have to go?
I feel I would be nicer if you were here.
I feel I could love, trust and show emotion if you were here.

Notice how often little children say, "Daddy, look what I can do." They use the power of acknowledgment in order to create a healthy selfhood. Later in life, it is this same call for affirmation,

"See me, notice me," that can become the balm for a

broken heart. In the times that we feel betrayed by our hopes and are faced with a life we never anticipated, we can be soothed by being accountable and receiving acknowledgment. We can find the strength and faith to absorb the steadfast shocks of life. When we hear a friend or parent say, "I know it hurts. I see that it hurts," we begin the liberation from our invisible worlds.

When I was having unsafe sex I lived a secret life. On the outside, I was one person; on the inside, I was somebody altogether different. I did not tell my therapist, my twin brother or my best friend where I was going on Monday nights. I never told my parents, my co-workers or any strangers about the dangerous ways in which I dealt with my issues. I simply lied. I would tell my roommate that I was going to a film and even read the reviews so that I could talk about it when I got home. In fact, on one particular Monday night, as the bus I boarded slowed down to its designated stop, I saw my alluring sex partner standing on one side of the street and my roommate standing around the corner. They occupied the same road that diverged and extended in different directions. My two lives were about to collide; the choice was mine to make. As I stepped off the bus I realized quite clearly that my secrets were my only true companions upon those intersecting roads. I did not want a witness, yet what I needed most was someone to really see me.

When I went for a battery of STI tests, I admitted that I was having unsafe sex.

"But only with one person," I added. The doctors didn't say, "Stop." They didn't say, "What's your problem? Are you crazy? Do you really hate yourself that much?" They didn't judge or condemn me. They didn't punish or shame me. They simply said, "Well, you're playing with fire, but it's your life." They allowed me to keep the autonomy that I suddenly no longer craved. They helped me to see myself as I was and, not liking what I saw, I lost the desire to ever have unsafe sex again.

That was it. My path of self-destruction ended on that day, at that minute, the instant I was finally able to recognize my behavior. As they held up a mirror into my secret world I thought, "Okay, I can make the changes now. I am accountable. I am ready to move on."

What if you want to help a friend who is not ready to make those changes? What if a friend, in becoming accountable, shares something that causes alarm?

My roommate, in my opinion, does not value herself. For example, she was set on the fact that she would not enter college being a virgin and did not. Since then, in three and a half years, she has had sex with a lot people, mostly unprotected. Each time was emotionally unsafe. A few of her partners have been men in their thirties; some are married and some have children. She claims that she "needs" sex. Recently she got in touch with an ex-boyfriend and told me, "I'm going to use him the way he used me!" Also, she smokes pot about five times a week; sometimes three times a day by herself. She is really faltering. I don't know if I can listen and stay unbiased anymore. I don't know if I can sit by and watch her destroy her life, while at the same time, I don't know if I can fight her from killing herself. You said that one thing people can do is listen. Well, I don't think I can anymore. And I don't know how to say "no" to her but I can't keep saying "yes" and condone that which she does. I don't know how to be a good friend to her and help her save herself. Mostly, I don't want to be the last support that walks away.
– Corey, age 20

It is never easy to watch while a friend has a finger on the self-destruct button. Once someone becomes accountable, how do you help if there is danger? To begin with, understand that helping someone is not the same thing as changing, stopping, fixing, lecturing, rescuing or altering him. We can't live another person's life. Your job is to assist, not to save. Your action is to supplement, support and nurture the fullness of another. Your goal is to guide a friend to find newer and deeper ways of loving him or herself. Often we spend so much of our time assuming other people's responsibilities or shielding them from the consequences of their actions. In so doing, we risk robbing them of the integrity of their experience and losing the focus on what is important for our own daily survival. A parent once told me, "I'm always trying to change my daughter to make her do what I want, and she resists. I think that as long I keep telling her I love her, it will be okay. But I see it's not. I need to hear what she is saying, to let her know she is seen and to work on really accepting her for who she is. We must allow people to be who they are when they are. Who am I to mold anybody?"

Here are six suggestions for helping a friend:

First: Be a demonstration. You inspire others by becoming a model of right action and lending a different perspective. Then they can see how it looks in the world and say, "I want to be like that." Become the example. Be the person who, for instance, does not have unsafe sex, nor lies to oneself and others and/or gets high three times a day. Every airline attendant instructs, in the case of emergency and the air bags are released from their overhead compartments, "Place the mask over your face first before assisting others." To be a demonstration is to be real and available. When people see that you are authentic, a person with principles and courage, they will want to be your friend. They will want a piece of what you've got, a piece of your aliveness.

Take all of your sorrow, grief and disappointment to make something that touches the lives of many people. Don't feel ashamed for being who you are.
– Marvin, age 10

The second rule I call, "The Ante-Up." In a game of poker it is the initial contribution that each person makes to the pot. In an

emotionally charged conversation this is the time for you to raise the stakes and make a contribution. To become trustworthy, you must trust others. To be the advisor, you must first allow yourself to be advised. Ask for your friend's support in something. Seek his or her counsel. Deliver your confidence to their command. Wager your own testimony. Share a similar story or secret about yourself they do not already know. Then gently offer a question like, "So, is it the same for you?"

We all have our pains and struggles and it takes reliance on
ourselves and each other to be well.
– Myeesha, age 17

Third: Develop effective communication skills. The greatest kindness
we can offer our friends is always the truth, especially when it comes from the heart. So when you want someone to hear your comments and feelings about their behavior, it is best to speak subjectively. Try using "I" statements: "I'm concerned. I'm afraid for you. I love you." In the words of one teenager to his girlfriend, "I feel your pain. It is mine also. Please let me help you." Pointing a verbal finger is usually not as effective: "You've got to stop. You've got a problem. You're headed for a fall." Always keep the concern coming from yourself. People can hear the word "I" much more easily than "You." It's a softer sound. It allows for feelings of safety and it's less likely to provoke defensiveness.

Language is my instrument of survival. Being an immigrant I appreciate
language, its nuances, capabilities and limitations. It is also my way of
having relationships with people.
– Dina, age 20

Fourth, as mentioned earlier, but worth repeating: If a friend is in
real danger, or if you think that is where a friend is headed, turn to an adult in whom you trust, even if they swear you to secrecy. Are you friend enough to risk losing someone in order to help?

We know it isn't easy being a teenager, and we also know that each of us
deserves the chance to live our lives without added complications.
– A high school guidance counselor

The fifth rule is usually the hardest to follow: Let go. Sometimes,
after you've tried everything, it is time to recognize that there is nothing

more to do. Some directions can't be reversed. Some trains can't be stopped. Some objects can't be fixed. Understand that over some things we are, in the end, ultimately powerless. A friend of mine once said, "I have changed the course of a couple of mighty rivers in my life. But some things, even after setting my virulent will to task, I can't change."

It takes pain and hurt to make us realize how fortunate we are.
That's how we grow. That is who we become.
— Miyuki, age 16

Finally, pray for your friend. Visualize and hope for a time that he or she will be surrounded by other people who are able to offer assistance. Continue to hope that he or she will find peace. And in your prayers, keep your heart open, for when you can see people in their true humanness, you can love anyone.

Maybe by showing my friends how much I love them, they'll think about
loving themselves enough to be careful with their bodies.
— Kim, age 16

Through it all, praise yourself for caring enough to want to find a solution. Your friends have chosen well if they have chosen someone like you who wants to make it easier for them. Commend yourself for your concern. Applaud yourself for your belief in all that is good in this life. And salute yourself for wanting your friends to be a part of such goodness.

If we could breathe life into other people and inspire them, then some
of the amazing energy that we pass to all those people must grow in us too.
We live through all the people we touch and in turn, just by the power
of thought, they live through us.
— Max, age 19

In the beginning of my seventh grade year, I found myself feeling
lonely and out of place. I felt like there was a world of difference
between me and my classmates. I was made fun of for taking school
seriously. No one else did homework, paid attention in class or
even passed tests. I was willing to do anything to fit in.

Anything, including humiliating another person. I started writing notes to a girl in my class who was picked on by everyone. I wrote that she should stop liking a certain boy (the leader of the whole "gang") even though she didn't like him. I wrote with my left hand and signed them, "Anonymous." With each note, I gained momentum. Each was nastier than the last. I had always been the angel girl with straight A's. All of the evilness inside of me came out in those notes. I vented on this poor girl. Finally, the guilt built up so much inside and I stopped. Then the principal found out and told my parents and they transferred me to another school. The whole ordeal was traumatic. Looking back, I guess I did it to feel accepted and loved. I was uncomfortable with myself and the way I was. I sacrificed my own safety and self-respect as well as destroyed an uninvolved, innocent person's self-esteem.
—Teresa, age 16

Become accountable. Take inventory of your character
and become responsible for making better choices in the future. In the words of Mara from Michigan, "I want so much for people to see that they are worthy and need to love themselves. Too many times I hear stories where people are making poor choices because they do not believe they are lovable. From this day on, I will honor my past and learn from my mistakes. Today is a new day, a new start and I am a new me."

When you see your breath on the first day of winter, look at the piece of your life force that emanates from within. As you exhale or speak into that first frost, pay attention to the proof of your presence in the world.

When you type an email to a friend, read what you have written before you press the 'Send' button. See your current existence on the screen before you. Take notice of how you are portraying yourself in that very moment.

When you empty your pockets each night, look at the day you spent. A day in the life of the things you collected: phone numbers, coins and new experiences. The things you used: money, ID cards or people. The things you held firmly: keys, coping mechanisms and hope.

Witness the imprint your life makes in this world and surround yourself with people who will vouch for your visibility. We are all living in a huge map of this world. Follow the arrow to the spot where it is written:

"You Are Here."

The Soldier at the bus stop

I am sitting at a bus stop on the corner of R'chov Gordon and Ha'Yarkon on a Friday morning in Tel Aviv. As I wait for the #4 bus to take me to the center of town, an Israeli soldier sits down beside me. He places his rifle on the bench between us and waits for his bus.

"American!" he suddenly declares, looking over at me. He takes the Walkman out of my hands and inspects it. "Sony," he says. "Very good." Then he asks, "Who are you?"
Are you a student or are you a tourist?"
Feeling somewhat indignant and eager to claim an identity,
I reply, "I am neither. I am a teacher."

The soldier seems to ignore my retort and begins to remove the batteries from the back of the Walkman. He inspects each battery, squinting to decipher the brand name printed along the seam.

"Panasonic. Also good," he says. "So! What do you teach?"

He holds a battery between his left thumb and forefinger. He studies it more carefully, heightening the awkwardness of two strangers sitting at an empty bus stop in the middle of the morning, in the meantime of their busy lives. I look on his face with fixed eyes, then down at the battery in his hand, and then back up at him. "HIV prevention," I answer.

As he replaces the batteries into the case and snaps the cover shut, I realize that all my favorite Israeli radio stations, which I had painstakingly pre-programmed into the machine, are now lost.

"Do you have it?" he asks. "HIV, I mean." He rests the Walkman in his lap.

"Yes," I reply.

He turns his face to look at mine. "Did you get it from having unsafe sex?"

"Yes, again." I reply.

He connects with my eyes. He waits a moment, then speaks. "Did you get it from having unsafe sex... with another man?" I answer his gaze by looking squarely into his eyes for a moment longer. "Yes."

The soldier at the bus stop gently returns my Walkman, as if he were handing me a gift. Then he forms his next sentence, carefully measuring each word. "There's something... I've always wanted to know... but have never had the chance to ask anyone before... so I'll ask you. Do you still... run?... Do you sweat... like the rest of us?... Do you... dance?"

I accept the Walkman, tendered from open hands and smilingly say, "Yes."

Instantly, his bus arrives, pulling up a few feet beyond the bench upon which we sit. Its brakes screech to a halt. He jumps up and lurches toward the sound of the door as it opens with a loud creak. With an exigent hunger, I watch as the soldier places one foot upon the first step of the bus and I fight against the feeling of sudden abandonment. Yet I feel forsaken and rejected, nonetheless.

Suddenly, he turns back, holds out his palm for me to see and with a kind smile says, "They say in the Israeli army that at night, if you listen carefully enough, you can actually hear the day burning."

And he is gone.

When I started college, my very first dance teacher on the very first day of class told us, "Today you will learn the most important thing about being a dancer." I stood at attention, in rapt delight, as I listened for her wisdom.

"Who are you? Hold out your hand," she commanded. "Show me your personality in the palm of your hand." I looked around at the rest of the students in class, all of us bewildered by her riddle. "Now show me your truth in your open hand. Let me see my wounds on your body," she continued, "that I might be reminded of my own truth."

I learned from my teacher that we are everywhere porous, that beauty cannot help but shine from our bodies and that we really don't have to do very much to be seen, to be beautiful, to be. She was trying to get us to understand that we dance when walking is not enough. We dance when God wants to see Himself on our bodies. We dance to feel connected to others. "Reveal yourself to me," my teacher instructed. "And in showing me your essence in the palm of your hand, heal me."

The next year in college, I had to declare a major that would supposedly prepare me for becoming someone who will one day do something in the world. Back then, I used to think that "who I am" is "what I do." If I practice law, I am as lawyers are. If I become a doctor, I am what doctors do. If I pursue dance, as I wished to, I would be what a dancer is. I will complete the mold and wear the uniform and fulfill the stereotype. And that will tell me who I am.

When I graduated from college I met James Bourne. James was a friend from the early days of AIDS. The last time I saw him, he was sitting on the floor of our Wednesday night HIV/AIDS support group in New York City, somewhere back in the first decade of the epidemic. He was wearing a colorful skullcap on his head and sporting an overgrown goatee. Frail and almost waif-like, his knees where hunched up to his chest as he spoke. "I can't walk as fast as I used to," he said. "I used to be able to put so much more into each day. Now it's just a struggle to get down the street. But suddenly I have all this time to see the flowers in front of me. I never saw them as I raced past, all those times before." In his dying, he was seeing so much more of life.

I am sitting at a bus stop on the corner of R'chov Gordon and Ha'Yarkon on a Friday morning in Tel Aviv. After two weeks of teaching all over Israel, I have become inured to the everyday details of life in Israel. Bank lines bore me and post office clerks bother me. I am beleaguered by beggars and homeless people. I am searching for a seat on the bus. I am late. I am fighting with cab drivers and switching to a better radio station on my Walkman. I am always on my cell phone. I am caught up in the minutiae of moments on Ben Yehuda Street or Kikar Tzion or the road from Jerusalem to my tiny hotel room.

Yet, as James Bourne taught me years ago, I am all that happens in the meantime of those moments. I am that which takes place in between what I think I am supposed to be doing and who I think I am supposed to be while doing it. And as my first dance teacher taught a few years before, I am the truth that I reveal and the reminder that heals. I am the connection I make with the people I meet. And finally, as the soldier at the bus stop taught me, I am the conversation on streets with strangers. I am the long stare into someone's eyes before I look away. I am he who is left behind with open hands, as someone I have just met and to whom I have laid bare my soul, runs to catch the next bus to anywhere new.

In the sage words of my friend Noa, "Everybody always says, 'How are you?' Yet people rarely say, 'Who are you?'"

I am sitting at a bus stop on a Friday morning in the meantime of my life. I am in between the moments of where I have just been and the anticipation of where I am headed. I am that which mindfully fills each day with meaning before it all too quickly burns away. ♔

Dear Scott,

My name is Eve and I'm a senior. I eat lunch at 2:44 every weekday afternoon—if you can call it lunch. That's when I come home from school and eat the bagel my mom makes for my lunch, a piece of fruit and anything until I get full. Stopping is always the hard part.

At first when the system was novel, I enjoyed just sitting in my kitchen with my own thoughts or with the mail or the newspapers, eating the bagel and an orange and then doing my homework. Those few minutes of relaxation were beautiful. Then, a few months later I got into a huge fight with one of my closest friends, ate too much pasta and beat myself up all the way through a slice of chocolate cake. I was so upset with myself for my gluttony and being so over-full that I went to the bathroom, leaned over the toilet and looked at my fingers to see if they would enter my mouth. I told myself I just wanted to get rid of the stomach ache but I knew I also wanted to get rid of the fat. I actually stuck my fingers inside and tried to gag myself, to induce vomit, but it didn't work.

This morning I woke up and ate a huge bowl of cereal because a huge bowl of cereal first thing in the morning is one of the most enjoyable, most comforting things ever. Then I went to school. At lunchtime I filled up my water bottle and sat with my friends. I am very conscious of the fact that

something
I'm extremely
ate it instead
being inside the
for so long

INVISIBLE KING
PM

I should be eating during the assigned lunch period with my friends to make them not notice that I don't eat; I'll drink instead. I'll say that I already ate during a free period or I'll try to pass it off with "I'm not hungry," or even something skimming the truth like "I'll eat at home." I remember one day when my best friend turned to me, asked where my bagel was, and I was so nervous that I actually went to my locker to get it, brought it back and had to start eating some of it. I was so upset that I had eaten it.

After school today, I planned on eating an apple and then setting out for a walk. But it's never that simple. I came home and looked at the fruit and decided to celebrate the good weather by eating a peach instead, my first this season. The peach was terrible, but the taste doesn't really matter. It's all about the texture and the mere experience of eating. Then I had some leftover pasta from Saturday night because I figured that at least it was healthy. But it left a spicy aftertaste in my mouth so I had a candy bar with chocolate, granola, raisins and almonds. Then I dropped my backpack in my room and saw a bag of the snack foods I took to the movies last night and brought it back to the kitchen.

Even though I was completely full,
I opened the bag of chips and decided
to finish them because there wasn't
that much left. I sat there for ten
minutes, maybe more, telling myself to stop
stuffing my face with chips that I don't even like.
But I finished the bag because I don't listen to myself.
Then I had a handful of chocolates in order to get
rid of the chip flavor. Then I got angry at myself because
I meant to only have one piece of fruit and go for a
walk but I didn't go because I kept eating and eating.

My mom, who always cooks meals and serves huge portions,
always tells me to eat more. And I'm not skinny.
I'm round, with a stomach that just appeared last year.
My dad always say things like "Don't snack on crackers.
Eat fruit and yogurt and not too much seconds. Drink
water, because juice has just as much sugar as a glass of
coke. And exercise! It's nice outside; go for a walk or a bike
ride. I'll buy you a pass to the gym if you'll use it.
Just take care of your body."

Sometimes I eat because I am hungry. Sometimes because
I think I deserve it. Sometimes just because it looks good.
Sometimes I eat because it's new and interesting and
sometimes because I am tired or bored.

Other times I'm just trying to prove to myself that I don't care at all what I eat or how I look. Sometimes I can't make myself stop eating until I feel nauseous or until my dad says something or until my friends leave the restaurant! It's crazy. I just compulsively keep eating. I know that I'm ready to stop but I just don't; the food tastes too good. Or maybe it's just that it feels so good to eat. I just can't stop eating and eating and eating.

No one knows I'm like this and I can't let anybody see because it doesn't fit in with who I am at all. I'm not materialistic or image-oriented. I don't participate in what I refer to as "skinny fashion." I encourage people to enjoy their bodies and be proud of who they are. I believe in fighting gender stereotypes and the destructive images from the media that permeate into our everyday lives. I'm always the kind of person who pushes friends to eat full lunches and be healthy.

THIS BEHAVIOR IS JUST NOT WHO i AM

My ghost returns to the kitchen at 2:44 every weekday afternoon. It reaches out its hand and I reach out mine.

— Eve, age 17

I feel very calm. Very centered. Very sad and very strong. I have never seen my own strength as something I could choose. Or even summon. Until now. I see the fork in the road and I can't completely believe that I have chosen the path of acceptance and peace over drama and blame.

I feel the world opening its arms to me, as to some beautiful princess who is meant to be free to use her whole heart.

— Jenny, age 30

5 | stillness

Daniel is a teenager who came up to me during a weekend workshop. With a big-toothed smile and his green baseball cap strategically turned backwards on his head he said, "I really like the talk you gave today. That really made me think." Daniel is adopted and his parents are in the middle of a bitter divorce.

"I want someone to love right now but I just don't trust love anymore after I've seen what my parents have done with theirs." He talked to me about living the "straight-edge life."

"When you are straight-edge like me, you know, no drugs or alcohol or sex, all the feelings you want to run from are right there in front of you. Always on your mind." He pointed to his forehead. "You can't escape them." He told me how he works through his problems by playing soccer, but that he is too hard on himself when he gives up a goal.

"Part of being human," I told him, "is not about playing the perfect soccer game or getting the highest grade in your class or even having the greatest sex with the greatest girl. It is about being able to sit in the center of your sadness and confusion, still knowing that you have worth. Understand that there is a difference between self-discipline and self-punishment."

"Yeah," he said, "I'm really hard on myself. I just want it to feel cool on the inside and I don't know how."

When you are in pain, when you are confused, when you don't know what to do, instead of overeating, putting your finger down your throat to throw up your dinner or not eating any food at all, cutting your skin, bullying someone else, not going to class, getting drunk, doing drugs, driving above the speed limit, having emotional and physical unsafe sex, showing up late wherever you go, living in unhealthy denial or any other destructive distraction, try this:

Just sit there.

Don't pick up the phone and call your best friend. Don't put in a DVD or watch TV. Don't judge yourself, forget about this moment and fall asleep on the couch. Don't do anything.

Just sit there.

Play your favorite music, shut the lights and sit in front of a candle. Create the scene, dress the part and begin. Decide to become an artist. Draw the outline of your pain and sit down inside of it. Or wrap yourself in your favorite sweater, walk outside underneath the sky and become mindful of the faithfulness of the sun. Even as it begins to recede from view, feel its warmth and know that it has been there all day. It is always there. You are not alone. Pain is God's way of pinching you so that you know you are still alive. Just allow. Just think. Just feel. You don't even have to cry.

Just be.

As I mentioned in the previous chapter, talking with someone else is always a great thing to do when you are in emotional pain. Just once however, don't. Simply sit and look at the carpet and get to know who you are as a person who is being visited with emotions. Because that is all emotions are: visitors. They are just colors that you paint onto the canvas of your unexplored worlds. They come and they go. They come to pass. They will change, lift and leave. But in the process, as you strengthen your inner emotional musculature, you can learn something from them.

Twenty-three year-old Greg says, "I find that when I sit in silence, I can hear the truth. I love the truth... whatever that is." Close your eyes, become familiar with silence and rummage through God's pockets in search of a scrap of salvation. In the middle of your confusion, your anger, your rage, in the center of your sorrow, your pain, your memories, at the core of your jealousy, your horniness and your fear, discover that you exist. Search for your truth. Know that you are worthy of carrying these feelings for a while. For just as you wish others to witness you, learn to witness yourself. This, to me, is strength.

I don't feel strongly toward things anymore. It's strange. My real best friend is who it always has been and probably always will be: Me. I don't know me perfectly, but I do know me better than anyone ever will.

I'm afraid of a lot of things, mostly of conforming in order to be liked.
I'm afraid I'm losing myself to an invisible enemy, that the door to my
mind is being closed by a powerful hand, stronger than mine. I have almost
everything I want yet I'm not content because I can't feel. Maybe I'm so
empty because I've changed so much. My mind has already expanded past
a certain point. I've dropped my old self somewhere, someplace I can never
retrieve it from. I can't go back again.
– Steven, age 16

When I was a teenager the mornings were often the most difficult time
for me, when I felt the potential for loneliness, the promise of the void
within. I too, was afraid of the emptiness, the feeling of being without,
of being alone in the world. And I was daunted by the craving to fill the
cavity in my chest. Though I have grown into an understanding and
self-accepting adult, it was not without years of searching so long for
others in relationships to role play and relive some of my earlier, painful
adolescent encounters. I searched for others to challenge and try to change
in order to redress some age-old sense of boyhood invisibility. I had unsafe
sex because I needed to do something. I thought I needed to medicate
myself, to get out of an emotionally fearful place, to detach from my
feelings, in order to be seen. I did not know how to just sit and be.

After I got infected, I was finally available to my deeper feelings and able
to work on my inner self. HIV for me was the wake-up call. It was the
snooze button on the alarm clock in my invisible kingdom that kept going
off, resoundingly saying, "Wake up! Deal with your life!" I had no other
option except to look inside. So I started the process of putting myself
back together again. In the stillness I began asking myself the question,
"Who am I?" And in the stillness I came to understand the answer. "I am
that which is beyond the brokenness and even the need for brokenness.
I am that which is valuable and blessed. I am infinite potential." At
one time these were just words, but sitting in the heart of my feelings,
I started to finally experience them. Over time, they began to actually
mean something.

There are times in your teenage years when you are going to want to do
anything to not feel your feelings. That is actually the very best time to
feel them. Just sit with them. Walk with them. Be with them. As sixteen
year-old Robbie from London puts it, "wrap yourself in a cloak of

stillness." Begin to trust what you know that you know deep in your soul. You don't have to do anything to deserve love.

You breathe. You belong. You are more than enough.

I no longer have the faintest idea how to identify the emotions that I feel, much less how to handle them. I can explain the sensation of chaos with the best of them, but couldn't tell you what it feels like to be sad as opposed to scared, or how to explain the difference between anger and loneliness. All I know is this sense of desperation from feeling whatever it is these emotions are. I'm stuck here in this kind of limbo: I want to medicate myself and deal with the emotions the only way I know how, i.e. doing something destructive. But I won't, so the feeling is even more magnified. It just sits there in the pit of my stomach and makes it impossible to pay attention in the classes I take that never fail to leave me feeling bored and cynical.
– Merisa, age 18

On every Israeli car is a bumper sticker that reads, in Hebrew, "Shmor Mirchak." Translated to English it means, "Guard your distance," advising other cars not to tailgate. On every train in the London Underground is a similar sticker that reads, "Mind the Gap," cautioning passengers to step carefully as they board the train. To me, they have another meaning: "Protect the space between." In between you and your own feelings is the space occupied by miracles. It is the place where you become accessible to healing. To be aware of this space is to be aware of the Divine. And the space is misleading in that it feels like emptiness. Guard it still. It is rich with possibility. It is the place each of us understands, whether we want to accept it or not. It is the seeming aloneness.

Guard it still. You are not alone. Even when it feels like others will never "get" you or see you or glorify the harrowing history of your heart. Even when it feels like you might drown in your tears, or be annihilated by your fears, or become lost within your loss. The inmost roads you travel are holy and though lonely you may be upon them, taking the journey of stillness is how you learn about yourself. It is how you learn that you exist.

My Resident Ghost

Never tangible, revealed in different forms
He's fleeting
Comes and goes, though transparent and open
(Sort of like me, sometimes)
I never have a clue of what he really wants
He's taunting me with empty promises
Forever just out of reach
But I will go with him blindly
Because I'm a naive, lost little girl with innocent eyes
Looking at a phantom for the first time
I just don't know any better
He's hovering over my shoulder and I can't escape
This apparition runs my life
I wonder if anyone else knows
My resident ghost
– Brianne, age 16

We all have resident ghosts. As you make peace with them in stillness, you will find an indwelling comfort. You are not alone.

The Girl outside the circle

the girl behind me
with her dirty feet and heavy eyes
remains a life preserver
tossed from a stable shore

she, collecting her change, is a fixed star
untouched in a changing constellation
spinning slowly above the waves
like the center of a record
to which I once knew all the words
   — Joel, age 16

While teaching at a camp in Massachusetts one summer, I sat in on a discussion group that was playfully called, "The God Seminary." The object of the session was to talk about the presence of God in our lives that week, or whether or not God even exists. But before we could begin, the rabbi leading the session asked for a prayer.

"Any prayer will do," he said. "We can't possibly begin a discussion on the existence of God without inviting Him in, can we?" I looked at the person to left of me who looked at the person to left of her and so on, but no one raised a hand.

"Surely someone must have a prayer," the rabbi said.
Still no one moved to speak.

Finally, he pointed to a young woman sitting on the couch outside of the circle, hiding from the rest of us. "You there," he directed, "sitting on the couch outside of the circle, hiding from the rest of us....you shall give us a prayer!"

"Me?" said the young woman, tensely. "I don't know any prayers. I... I... don't know."

"We will wait," answered the rabbi. "If we learn nothing else today, we will have at least learned from you. We are in search of the presence of God and we need your prayer to find it."

So the girl outside the circle looked down at her shoes and up at the group staring back at her; then down again at the floor and once again up at us. Her face had reddened, her eyes filled with tears and with hesitation, her mouth opened to speak.

"I don't know," she said.

"That's your answer?" asked the rabbi, smiling. "I don't know."

"I don't know," repeated the girl, apologetically.

"Aah," said the rabbi. "That's the perfect prayer... the perfect prayer."

Dear Scott,

This summer Jake and I got together. He was a guy that I wanted forever, but never thought it would happen. However, it finally did. We were together for three weeks before the summer ended; we were inseparable. We knew long distance relationships were bad, but decided to stay together anyway. I totally knew we had this special bond. We spoke on the phone for like three hours every night without fighting once. It was so nice.

We had so much in common and were so comfortable with each other. I usually feel kind of awkward around guys, but not him. We stayed together for two more months and everything was still wonderful. After a while, we began to talk about having sex. I said that I was concerned he would break up with me right afterwards. He told me that he would never do that. He never loved anyone more than me, but if I wasn't sure about the sex, then we wouldn't do it. Both being virgins, we were very nervous, but deep down I knew that it would be alright.

At the end of September, I went to visit him and we had sexual intercourse. It was amazing; I felt this awesome bond with him. It seemed like he did, too. But when I came back home, I called him and he was really rude. In fact, he was rude for the next week. He had never acted like this before. When I brought it to his attention, he said I was being annoying and he could not handle a long distance relationship anymore. He said that it was too hard to be away from me. I told him that he should have thought about that before he had sex with me. He said he knew that and he wished he could take it back. This was all about two weeks ago. He hasn't called since.

I just don't know what to do. We were so in love. Neither of us had ever felt this way before. I cannot believe he would have sex with me and then break up with me. I never thought anyone could be such an asshole, you know? He took something from me that I can never get back and I do not know how to handle it. I do not know if he still has feelings for me or still loves me. I am just so hurt and I don't know what to do. He doesn't understand how much he has hurt me. I tried to explain it to him, but that just seemed to make matters worse.

I miss him and I miss what we used to have. I feel stupid that I lost my virginity to him and then he turned on me. It was like he got scared and did not know what else to do. This was his first serious relationship. What we had was so amazing. How do I remind him of that?

— Rachel, age 17

Letters from the
Secret Lives of Teens

Why to love.

Because when I'm driving back from somewhere
I don't want to leave, and a song comes on the radio
that suddenly feels like it's melting into my soul,
and the sun is starting to recede, I race against it so
I can run inside and not see it, and then it won't ever set.
Because time is my greatest commodity and I'll give it
up for you. Because I'll beg, "Stay up late and tell me
too much and pretend I'm the only important factor in
your busy overachiever life for just these few hours and
be drunk on me and mean it when you ask how I am and
answer me truthfully when I ask how you are and
love me back. Just please love me back."
— Audrey, age 21

6 | surrendering

A few years ago in a high school cafeteria somewhere in America, a teen-ager pointed his step-father's handgun at five of his classmates and shot them. He then walked out of the building and onto the softball field, knelt down in the grass and put the gun in his mouth. Before he could pull the trigger the assistant principal somehow convinced him to drop the gun. As he fell into his teacher's arms he said three words, which were printed in bold red ink as a special report in Time magazine the next day:

"I'm so scared."

A few nights earlier his girlfriend broke up with him.

Mimi was sitting on a bus looking up at a stretch of sky through the window. "What fascinates me most," she said, "is that no matter where in the world you are, everyone looks up at the same night sky." Mimi is a teenager from Milwaukee who gave up her virginity to her high school sweetheart. "I love you so much," he told her. "**And if we just do this together, I promise I will never leave you**." So she did. And then he did. Sharing a seat with me on a two-hour bus ride to Chicago one late Saturday night she told me some of her story. "Why do guys have to say they'll never leave?" she asked plaintively, looking away from the sky. "I wish they would never say it or just never leave. How am I going to live with the memory of this?"

Whenever she remembers the pain of rejection, "I pick up a razor blade and proceed to put tiny little slits all the way up the underside of my left arm, marveling at how good it feels the entire time." She tried to show me some of her scars, but the passing lights on the highway were not bright enough to sufficiently illuminate our seat on the bus in our tiny corner of the world. "I blame it all on me and then resort back to hurting myself."

"When you cut," I inquired, "What do you feel? Not in the moments you are preparing to cut. And not in the moments afterward when you are cleaning up. But in the very moment that you see the blood coming out of your arm, Mimi, what are you feeling?"

She thought about it for a long time; indeed, no one before had ever asked her such a question. Finally she spoke. "In those moments, when I see the blood, I feel three words: 'One More Day.' I realize that I can go on one more day." She looked out the window of the bus for a second while gathering her words. "I guess I thought I would have grown out of the whole teen angst thing, as my mother so helpfully refers to it, by now. Instead, it only seems to be getting worse. I just can't stop cutting!"

Later in the year, Mimi sent me an email:

I don't want to be another snotty nose teen asking you for help with my poor little life, but I want to cut a lot. I'm lonely and depressed and that frustrates me. I want to be normal yet I feel like I'm going crazy. I feel worthless. I don't trust people. It scares me to think I would be allowing someone into my world. My parents hide all sharp objects in the house and stuff. Sometimes my mom will just stare at me and then say, "God, what have you done to yourself? Just look at your arms! Awful. Just awful!" I don't know...couldn't I just keep doing it and end up fine? What's the worst thing that could happen? Seriously. I just can't remember feeling any other way besides this...I mean, when I cut myself it hurts, but I feel better. I'd like to believe there are other things I can do to make me feel better, but I can't seem to find out what those things are. Plus, in my head, I'll always want to cut. You see? I want to believe that I can let someone inside my world. Most of all, I want to believe that I deserve kindness.

A pediatric nurse once instructed me on this subject.

"Self-mutilation is a way of not committing suicide," nurse Joan told me. "If you take
it away, you take away a survival option." Teenagers, both male and female, cut for many reasons. For Mimi and others like her, self-injury becomes a fix, the hook that pulls them in, helping them to get through a crisis. It's a way to access the pain, to be out of the pain or even to protect the pain. One writes, "For me, it's about willpower and being proud of myself that I can withstand the pain." Some cut to calibrate the chaos on the inside with the confusion and disorder on the outside: "I was just so unhappy with myself that I'd do anything to harm myself." Some

cutters wear their wounds like a shawl that both protects and draws attention to them. Yet while some, in an appeal for attention, want to show the world they are hurting, the proverbial 'cry for help,' most want to hide their scars and bury their bruises. "I cut myself on my chest," writes one. "It's the only place I know I can do it without people seeing." Some do it as a way of rejecting help when it seems that people don't take their pain seriously enough. "I honestly don't think I deserve to be listened to or cared for." Some cut to recondition their shameful thinking. "Every time I see a good-looking guy," writes one male teen, "I want to hurt myself, so I burn my skin." For others, there simply is no other option. "I cut because physical pain starts and ends," says Amanda, "but emotional pain just goes on and on." One parent who works the late shift on a teen helpline said, "between midnight and four am, that's when the cutters call. They want me to convince them not to cut, to prove to them that life is not only about pain." With only their mournful ghosts for company, they remain alone on the island of self.

Whatever the reason, the scars of self-affliction are

more than mere marks left behind by the healing of injured tissue. They are skin graffiti, the artistic depiction of bitter things. They are emblematic of the internal inferno, tangible evidence of feeling unworthy. They both document the inner emptiness and actually become the infinity of empti-ness within. They are, themselves, the vacancy and the void made visible.

When life gets reckless with us, we sometimes get reckless with ourselves. We take revenge on the closest thing to us: our bodies, our lives and our futures. How do we prepare for a broken heart? How do we live with such a loss? Whose arms can we fall into? When we look toward tomorrow we think, "Is it always going to be this way? How will I survive this parting?"

Oftentimes in life, there is a strong need for the sheer presence and beauty of hope in every way and in every moment. This is one of those times. It takes a while to become adept at allowing for life's unexpected but faithful aches. It is never easy learning to make room for the casualties of love. Allow yourself to be sad. Lather yourself in loneliness. The inmost roads are stretched before you; the search within can begin. Undefended from pain and so very much alive, in a strange and horrible way, you are about to be touched by grace.

Learn from your woundedness. Though you
may hide it from others, never hide it from yourself. Open your fists and surrender. And sit. And ache. And say to yourself, "Here I am with open hands, emptied of the arms they once held. This is my broken heart." Don't vanquish it. Don't fight it. Don't fix it. Take to the trembling. Cave in to the craving. Accept the fact that a heart, once broken, can never truly be repaired. If it could, the sadness you feel today would be felt in vain, and the lessons you gather from this experience would decrease in value.

The lessons are important.

Think about your courage. Think about your willingness to feel all of life. This is what it means to be alive. It's not just breathing, but thriving, really living. Emotional pain is a great teacher. Do not hurry to dishonor its presence in your life. In the future, people may turn to you in silent deference because they know in some way that you have traveled upon the terrifying terrain of the human heart. And it will help them.

You need your pain. Others can learn from your pain. Make room for it.

I could tell you that I'm doing okay, but the truth is, I'm not. Every time I start to think that I'm doing a bit better, I keep thinking of her. I miss her so much but I can't pick up the phone to call her. I want to tell her how I love her and need her now. I can't get her smile or laugh out of my mind for a second. And yet, I'm filled with so much confusion, too. I think I'm still in a lot of shock. The last thing I want to hear is, "There are other fish in the sea," not when the only thing I want is her. So I put on an act in front of everyone. No one asks me how I'm doing anymore cause I guess I do a great job acting okay. But no matter how hard I try I can't stop thinking about her and the experiences we had. Part of me says this is just a phase she is going through, but another part of me says that I've already lost her to someone new. And another part is completely scared.
– Nathan, age 19

The loss of love turns into famine. Once tasted, however briefly, no crumb is left uncraved from love's table. In the aloneness, you hunger for the tiniest piece of that which nourished you each day. Yield to that scarcity.

Mangled in the memory of that final

embrace, you may find yourself picking at the wound in pursuit of its origins. Allow for it. Hold on to it until the time comes that, from out of this pain, you can create something beautiful.

The passing of months may find you still longing for the privilege of their company. You might miss them in your favorite meeting places or in the emptiness on the spot where beside you, they once stood. That very space, having once claimed their closeness, might seem to miss them, too.

This past 4th of July I started a very special relationship with a guy who loved the way my hair smelled and who looked into my eyes as if he was looking at what was just beyond them. In his words, "The time we spend together is perfect." Then I learned that he kissed another girl. A kiss, to me, is a beautiful and passionate thing that you only give to someone whom you really care for. After finally being convinced that I was someone who could be cared about in that way, to have that trust broken is unimaginable. This is more than just a teenaged relationship glitch; it's the way his actions have shouted over his words and drowned out my emotions. I am searching for that part of me inside that will survive all hurt. I am looking for guidance to hold onto when my heart won't hold on. I want to keep my face to the sun so I'll never see the shadows. Is there really beauty in everything?
– Danielle, age 16

There is much to learn from the underside of love, from the depths of the emotion within. Loss, unbidden, teaches that all things are connected, that future joy is burdened with ancient tears. Where there is comfort there is also pain. And in the stillness after the weeping, the ground beneath your feet becomes a little softer, receiving the weight of your sorrow, sharing in the burden. Then are you truly inside of mercy's shadow and able to know that you are being taught the full nature of your sustenance and introduced to your amazing strength.

Edward is a teenager who recently went through a breakup. "I feel like I need to take his pictures down off the wall," he wrote. "But I don't want to stop seeing his face." Each of us is at risk of having a broken heart. It takes great courage to believe in love; to believe that love is worth the cost of breathing; the price of the pulse of blood in your veins; the gathering of a million mornings of hope.

In the words of one teen, "In the moment you pledge your highest love, you greet your highest fear. For the first thing you worry about after saying 'I love you' is whether you'll hear it back. In love, I see everything that lives. Love is stillness; a stillness which is the ground from which all other things arise. In this love, I become who I must understand." It is a holy thing to love what can change. It is a courageous thing to love what can leave. Only the brave of us, who were once the lonely of us, have the courage to sink deeply into that huge mess called relationships, undefended from pain and unarmored from joy. Salute yourself. For to love another is to summon your loneliness and temporarily cast it to the waters. Thus, it feels heavier and more acute once it returns, as it washes up against the shoals of your heart from a deeper ocean within you, long held at safe distance. And again, you are filled with emptiness.

Wouldn't it be something if we could stop, lean in and let ourselves
be carried inward? Deep to the center of our inhabitance.
The windows would no longer be curtained. Then we might be able to
see what stood there all along.
– Peggy, age 18

After a while, you will learn to grow accustomed to the calmness that comes from sorrow. You will become aware of the value of not just days, but hours. And you will come to believe that it is the plea itself, not the answer to your plea, that heals. Believe that believing is enough, at least for today. Perhaps there is no greater meaning or truer lesson from all your unhappiness than that which is found by simply granting yourself permission to feel your sorrow.

Read that sentence again.

You will come to learn that some things can not be fixed. You will become acquainted with a deeper sense of self, a self devoid of poetry or style, personality or charm. A self that does not have all the answers, or any answers. Though others will tell you that time is a healer, in an unconventional way, you might even hope that you always stay a little bit broken. Because somewhere in these seemingly ungraceful moments you will become acquainted with a self that is truly in grace.

Love is not dispensable.

It keeps disguising itself and reminding us of life's possibilities. Take all the time you need. You have met and been nourished by the soul beneath your skin. Empty your suitcases and hang your sorrows in the closet, alongside your joys. Settle in for a season of grieving. A season of growing. When neither sadness nor joy is eclipsed by the other, then you will know what it means to be truly alive.

I run through blackness, yet under heaven's light
I sing to stars so they hear me this night
I pray for love that it may show itself soon
This is my prayer as I run under the moon
– Adam, on his 15th birthday

Ancient Aunt Edith

I remember my Aunt Edith. She was sitting next to me in the backseat of my grandfather's gray two-door, 1967 Oldsmobile F/85 sedan with the red vinyl seats and matching felt ceiling. We were driving through Forest Hills on the way to the beauty parlor in the summer that I was seven. My twin brother was sitting up front and, as always, Aunt Lil was driving.

"How about we stop for some ice cream?" Aunt Edith asked. "The boys want some ice cream." How did she know? How could she tell that my tongue was craving a chocolate-dipped cone from the Carvel stand on the side of the road? How could she see so much of what I could barely realize I myself desired?

"No" Aunt Lil said. "We don't have enough time to stop."

"But why not? Let's just stop for a minute," Aunt Edith urged, unsuccessfully defending my silent quest. "It'll only take a minute... for the boys."

"They don't want any ice cream," Aunt Lil said to Edith, speaking into the rear view mirror.

Unyielding, she sighed, "It's just a little ice cream for the boys."

This was amazing to me. I felt as though I had started a fight and I hadn't even opened my mouth. I was torn. I knew it was too late to advocate on my own behalf. If Aunt Edith couldn't do it, how could I? And I was mortified that the muted yearning of something which seemed so silly was causing such a stir.

Mostly, though, I was horrified for not having come to my Aunt Edith's defense; having abandoned her, I somehow felt responsible for getting her in trouble. So I just sat there and never said a word, pretending that I really didn't want the ice cream anyway. As I turned to look out the window, I watched the Carvel stand disappear into the lost landscape of Queens Boulevard.

Those unrequited longings in summer moments of long ago have cultivated a generosity within me. I think that I am going to resurrect more memories of ancient Aunt Edith and assemble them into the perfect nurturing mental bodyguard. I will call her "Aunt Elixir" and she will never accept "no" for an answer. No longer will I bear shameful secret cravings for things unaskable, like ice cream, attention and other dangerous daydreams.

She will belong to the "C'mere People," a loyal legion of merciful individuals whose sole job it is to defend and nurture the places inside ourselves where we hide. I will listen for her calling out, and this time she will get her way in defense of my ineffective entreaties.

"Come to me," she'll say. "Come here." And she'll press my face under the canopy of her bosom, covering my ears with her hands, shutting out the noise of the sometimes intimidating world I inhabit.

Standing sentinel over the loneliness of silent longings, she will defend my invisible kingdom. ♔

Dear Scott,

I first knew I was different when I was in 6th grade. I looked at all the other kids and listened to what they were saying. And I knew I wasn't the same as them. Most people say that in grammar school you are too young to understand, but I knew I was different. That was the first time I developed a crush on another guy. Back then, I fabricated two different realms of living: one of fantasy and one of reality. The two were totally independent from one another. All through junior high school I lived this life. The life of a lie. Soon the time had come when these once independent worlds would collide. I was at a sweet-sixteen party when I saw a young gay couple dancing together. They were holding hands and having a good time. All of a sudden I had an epiphany, a sudden realization: what they are is what I am — what I want to be.

I began asking myself questions. Out of the six billion people in the world, why me? Why am I different? What does it mean to be gay? Why God, why did you do this to me? What is the value of my living if there is nothing but pain and suffering? Why do I exist? I felt completely isolated. I had no one to talk to. I was afraid of rejection, of people turning their backs on me just when I needed them most. I was afraid that they would

break my trust and wouldn't see that my being gay is not an entire identity, but only a part of who I am.

I told no one of this self-realization, but endured the pain every waking moment. I began to write poetry, my escape from the torturous thoughts that pervaded my soul, undermining the infrastructure of my identity. i HAD NO iDENTiTY. Everything I lived was a lie. I was not a person, only a false representation of a human being with physical features and a name. All that I had been taught was crumbling at the very existence of one piece of knowledge. It was as though once the sun began to shine on my life my whole world became dark.

In my junior year, I told my secret to a guy that I liked for three years. I thought I could trust him. He told the track team, most of my friends and eventually people I did not even know. I couldn't bear walking down the halls of my high school because people screamed "fag" or

whispered behind my back. The looks of disgust burned a hole right through me. I wanted everything to disappear. I wanted to die. Thoughts of suicide rampaged through my head. Every waking moment I would think of the easiest and fastest way to end my life. I couldn't sit through a period of chemistry without thinking, "No one is going to be at home later. I can do the deed tonight."

One day after school I went home, walked straight into the kitchen and got a knife. I brought it to my room and laid it next to me on my bed. I sat for hours on end, blankly staring at it, seeing the reflection of a worthless human soul in the sharp blade. I drew it near to my skin wishing the pain would all go away. I carved the word FAG into my leg. I thought it would alleviate some pain. It didn't.

These are the dreams I want to accomplish:
To have someone look me straight in the eyes and say,

"I know your secret. I care about you."
To find someone who will call up just to let me
know that they are thinking about me.
To be in the presence of someone that can see inside me
and know and feel everything I have felt.
To experience everything, the love, pain and joy
that everyone goes through.

I want to live, experience, BE!
I have not accomplished any of these.
I have been waiting for that moment for so long,
day in and day out.
All I want is for someone to care.

        — Chris, age 19

The one thing that we as human beings desire the most is also the one thing that we as human beings fear the most: to open up to one another and let each other see ourselves for who we really are. Every person has a story to tell but very few opportunities to tell it. In order for a person to "come out" in any way, he or she needs someone to come out to.

As a gay youth, there was no one I could talk to in the town where I grew up. A lot of people did not want to hear what I had to say. So I looked to the Internet and chat rooms to find people to ask how they got through it. Most of the time this led to chatting with men, knowing that it would only be a few more minutes, and a few more words, before they stopped listening and started asking about my looks, my sexual experiences and when I wanted to meet in person. Even though I never met any of them, I wanted to know what it felt like to be taken care of by another man, to be held, and most of all for another man to see me, all of me, and love what he saw.

— Brian, age 19

7 | coming out

When my friend Fred was a little boy in the 1960's in Cincinnati, Ohio, his family got a brand new typewriter. After everybody tried it out, it was finally Fred's turn, because he was the youngest. So he sat down to plunk out some words and typed a letter to his best friend, Billy.

"Dear Billy, I love you."

His father, looking over his shoulder, pulled the paper out of the carriage and ripped it up, saying, "You can't love another boy."

Jeremy's face was starting to show signs of adolescence. When I first met him a few years ago, his skin was clear and hairless and he carried a ready expression in his smile that told me when he was about to deliver another discordant joke. I remember when he proudly donned his Bert and Ernie slippers and announced to everyone that they were his "first gay role models."

When I saw Jeremy a year later, his forehead was bespeckled with tiny red acne scabs and there was some peach fuzz above his upper lip. His eyes turned away from mine as he sat in the front row of one of my lectures. He seemed to be searching for something off in the distance. Jeremy had lost his smile.

After my talk, he shared his story. Earlier in the summer he attended a beach party where a guy his age, by whom he was besotted, asked him to join on a walk. After a few minutes, he turned to Jeremy and told him to

"suck him off."

He declined at first, but when the guy protested lightly, it didn't take much to get Jeremy to acquiesce.

"I always wondered what it would be like to do that for the first time. I didn't enjoy it. I wanted it to be over with," Jeremy told me, his cheeks effusing a semi-permanent adolescent blush. "It wasn't the way I wanted it to be."

Then his mother read about the experience in his diary and forbade him to leave the house. Somehow, over time Jeremy was able to meet another young man from a town not too far away and forged his first gay relationship. On New Year's Eve he felt that things were happening too fast and that this new boyfriend was too needy.

"I know I'm gay, but I'm not ready to be in love," he said to me. "So I had this guy's parents drive me to a friend's house about thirty minutes away. I never saw him again. I lied to my parents about everything. And there's more..."

Jeremy started doing drugs. "Just Ecstasy," he defended. "The 'happiness drug.' Don't you see?" he said, defining himself by adversity, "I have to prove to my parents that I will never be who they want me to be."

What does it mean to "come out?" Come out of what? Society assigns it an erroneous metaphor: "the closet." However, a closet is not large enough. There are too many thoughts, emotions and sensations involved in the process of growing up with secrets to fit into a mere closet. There is hidden shame, clandestine love and unresolved struggle. There are silent crushes, furtive glances and unrequited longings. There is denial. There are years of defamation, self-rejection and abuse all buried beneath the truth of our dreams. No closet can adequately subsume these experiences. Rather, it is an invisible kingdom of unfulfilled and inglorious yearning, an entire realm of confusion, a universe of mercilessness.

Standing in the vulnerability and insecurity of adolescence is painful, yet it is seminal to a life of courage. When I was growing up, people rarely stepped forward to say, "Whatever you are feeling is okay. There is a place for you in this world." Instead, by the time I got to high school, I heard people pontificating that "homosexual feelings are really a man's fear of a relationship with a woman," and "You're confused because you don't feel masculine. If you'd start working out, you'd become the man you think you are looking for." Or worse, "it's a choice." I even remember reading a book on sex where the definition of a homosexual was "any man who is obsessed with the genitals of another man." As long as I did not think about anything beneath the belt of another guy, I believed I was normal.

With every day, a little neglect. With every neglect, a little more self-denial. Day by day, I dug a moat around my invisible kingdom, until I, myself, did not know how deeply ensconced I had become.

Very often we think that after we have "come out" we never have to do it again. But that is not the case. People struggle every day. Lesbian, gay, bisexual, transsexual, transgender, intersex, queer or straight identified people struggle with their identity all the time. But so does everyone else. We are all attempting to come out to ourselves and each other with our life experiences, be it as a person with AIDS, as a person who has been raped or sexually assaulted, as an individual with an eating disorder, a person who struggles with depression, adoption issues or someone living an unfulfilled life. The list could go on.
– Brian, age 19

Everybody has a secret, and not necessarily one sexual in nature. Each of us feels that we are different from the rest of the crowd. Have mercy on yourself. Underneath all the inside information, we have many things in common. We look different; we have dissimilar experiences; we have distinct beliefs which take us to alternative places and offer us varied life circumstances. But we all have the same desire to be witnessed, accepted and loved unconditionally. In the final analysis, **we can celebrate our differences and tell the same truth.** Sometimes, underneath the fear of someone who is different is a desire to connect with that someone who is different. What would that connection feel like? In the absence of such fear can exist a wealth of innocent joy.

Sometimes I am transgender. Sometimes 'trannyboi.' Sometimes I even feel 'grrly.' Mostly I choose to be sexual in a gender-free manner. I love fems, butches and 'wimmin.' I have fallen in love with bio-boys and 'tranny-boiz.' If I wanted, I could say I'm a straight boy or a straight girl. But who cares to be 'Str8?' I have the best of all worlds. Do we have to pick a gender identity to love someone? I think we all have the right to own our identity. I choose not to limit my capacity to love or how that love manifests itself. Don't choose my identity for me.
– Pony Boy, age 16

You do not choose your secrets. Your secrets choose you.

Understand the difference. Regardless of your secrets, you are not a criminal, a bad person or an embarrassment. You are not a textbook that others can read. You are not a scientific experiment of which anyone can ask rude, invasive and inappropriate questions. You are not an unredeeming, one-dimensional, underdeveloped character in an overrated television show. You are not a phenomenon.

As my friend Leslie says, "The best things about a person are on the top shelf of their closet." You are real. You are here. You are an important and valuable person. And like anyone else, you live with contradiction and confusion. Embrace your story. You have done nothing wrong. I write these words because I needed to read them myself years ago. Lying naked in bed with another man for the very first time, I said to myself,

"I can't allow this secret life. I can't enjoy my

wrongful desires. I can't accept this." In the heat of the moment, I wanted to hurt myself with unsafe sex. As one teen explains, "I wanted a glimpse of the world of closeted men, whose true nature so few actually know."

I am consumed with a dream where I can stand next to you
*   and not be judged*
Where I can love and not be mocked
Where my words are wasted because there is equality
Where my struggle is an illusion because there are no barriers
Where you and I are friends and no one cares where we can hug
I am consumed with a dream where homosexuality is as scandalous as cheese
Where my desires are as common as yours
Where image is not as important as inner beauty
I am consumed with a dream
And I never want to wake up
– Mike, age 18

Before you can divulge your secret life to another, you must first reveal it to yourself. Coming out to yourself tests and strengthens your emotional musculature. Let it. Speak to yourself of love and courage. Speak to yourself of a better life. Whisper the words into the ear of your heart, "I am valuable. I am likable. I am good."

A wise old rabbi once said, "When I die, God will not ask, 'Rabbi Zusya, why were you not like Moses?' He will ask, 'Why were you not Rabbi Zusya?'" While it may not be easy, start by asking "Why not?" Why not be you? **Why not be proud?** Why not live up to your magnificent, absurd and exultant potential?

Keep returning to the insubordination of refusing to be suppressed, however irreverent and stubborn that seems. You are merely trying to hear and honor the true voice within. To be fully alive you must notice yourself. **Shine. You are here and you matter.**

Everyone always says, "Stay true to yourself." Well, I realized at the beginning of this year that I'm gay. This is who I am. Although many do not accept my lifestyle, I can't provide for everyone. To me, not being yourself is like cheating on a test: you never know if you're going to fail; it all depends on who you copy.
– Collin, age 15

Many years after I came out to my parents, my father said to me: "I love you more and more each day because I am learning whom it is I love." Ultimately, we have very little control over how others feel or talk about us and accept who we are. You are not in this world for the approval of others. What people say and think about you is none of your business. Your job is to discover a compassion of self that you may never have embraced in lifetimes before. Your role is one of self-acceptance, not self-improvement. You are perfect. It is an inner embrace, a constant quest for self-soothing. A softening. Do not be afraid to face your authenticity. Listen to it as it summons you. Your true path awaits upon the inmost roads.

I am in awe of your courage.

I had a voice teacher who taught: "The most visible creators I know are the artists whose medium is life itself. They express the inexpressible. Whatever their presence touches increases life for **they are the artists of being alive."** The strange and wonderful gift of all this inner torment is that one day you will be able to genuinely and unquestioningly love yourself out loud. It will emanate from within you, deep inside, from a place of knowingness. Nothing anyone can ever say, do or ask of you will ever change the simple truth of your awe-inspiring existence. You have the same rights as anyone else. Continue to believe in yourself and all of your steadfast dreams and wistful imaginings.

I am far from the stereotypical gay male and that can be very hard for me at times. Being a varsity captain of the soccer and tennis teams, a good student, a gentleman and a rather good-looking guy (so I have been told), I feel I could change a lot of minds about how gay people are perceived. It's very hard for me to meet other people like myself at my age because many of them are going through the same uncertain stage I am. As I continue to live my life as a young gay man, I know there will be many challenges to overcome along with many joyous and comforting events. I am not afraid to be who I am anymore and I refuse to ever let myself return to such a stressful state of mind and heart. I am who I am. I'll be who I want to be and I will always know within myself that it is okay. If anyone else ever reads this email and is going through the same sort of situation, I just want to say that there will always be someone in your life who cares about and supports you and that there is never a good enough reason to fear being the person you are and want to be.
– Tim, age 17

A college freshman came out to his parents over his winter break. "If I taught you how to throw a baseball when you were a kid," the father asked, "would that have made a difference?"

"Yes," said the son, "then I would have been a gay guy who knows how to throw a baseball."

Be who you are.

The Alternative Kids

It is early Monday morning, the uneasy start to another week of high school. Filing first into the classroom my bright-eyed students enter throwing their bookbags under their appointed seats. Following behind are the friends on phones with after-school plans. Arriving last, the bleary-eyed stragglers with time to squander. A beginning to another week of high school in the middle of anywhere.

Though I have been summoned here and to the city before this, and the one before that, it is not without my own mix of loneliness and resistance. I am spent and exhausted from the miles I have traveled; I belong to the road. I already feel embattled from the emotions that will come out of me when I finally begin to speak. One by one, as the students take their seats, I prepare myself for another long day of lectures. The end-of-autumn air wafts through an open window and I look out onto a leaf-strewn street. A sign catches my attention: "Hope Street." Suddenly, what at first feels like doubt now becomes faith. Faith turns into words. Words into healing. At once I remember why I have come.

I have come to meet Mary, whose eyes are gray and unfocused. She looks down at the floor as she talks, except when she laughs.

When she laughs, she throws her head back and commands all eyes upon her. Mary laughs a lot. But right now she is telling us about a man who died of AIDS, a friend of her mother's. "I was unhappy about it... when I found out," she says. "I mean, even though I didn't really know him, I still felt something for him, you know?" Sitting in the front row, she listens to all my stories. She observes with her face, not with her eyes. She asks questions without raising her hand.

"Mary?" I inquire, as if somehow her name has become a question. "Can you see me?" Looking up from the floor, searching in the direction of my voice and studying the space I occupy, she answers. "Not really. Well, kinda. I mean... I can make out some shadows. Sort of."

Upon confirming for myself that she is blind, I explain to the class that the thing that always shocks a room is being able to see me; to see how healthy I look in spite of the news that I am HIV positive. "To see that I have good taste in clothes," I add. They all laugh, Mary the loudest. "That's how you start to know me and to feel comfortable with me." And I explain that Mary cannot do that. "But you can feel my words, can't you?"

She looks down again, nods her head and smiles. "I can feel you," she reiterates. "I can feel you."

Today I am teaching one hundred and fifty students in an alternative high school in the middle of the country. These are the "misfits" of their community, the ones who need extra attention. "The valiant ones," as I describe them. "You have found a way to declare your differentness and seek a sense of belonging. You have succeeded. Only, it is not enough," I continue. "You must share your stories with the world. If you can live out loud, live louder. If you can dress this boldly, dress bolder. If you have something to say, we want to hear it."

Alden is part of an acting troupe that's putting on a play about the life of Harvey Milk, the first openly gay person to be elected to the Board of Supervisors/City Council in San Francisco. Eleven months later, in 1978, he was assassinated. "I'm feeling a little weird about it," Alden tells me over a late breakfast consisting of a bagel, two waffles, jalapeno-flavored potato chips and a neon green can of over-caffeinated soda. "I mean, we have to perform it for the kids at the other school."

"The other school" is the mainstream high school Alden used to attend, or rather, fled from, because he felt unsafe for being different. "For being gay," he says. "And now I'm going back to perform this show and it's kind of... weird."

I try to get him to see the growth in it: "You won't be alone on that stage, Alden. You'll be surrounded by your new friends, people who understand you because they are just like you."
I point out the poetic irony: "Those very students you once fled from - you now get to teach."

"Yeah, I guess," he says. "But it's still kind of weird."

Yesterday I spoke at that mainstream high school only a half-mile away. When I mentioned to them that I would be speaking to "the alternative kids" tomorrow, they started an incendiary murmur. Some of the students whispered while others laughed. Some even hissed.

"They feel the same way about you," I uttered impulsively. It was a risk. For a split second, in the silence after, I wondered if I had gone too far, until suddenly a huge roar of teenage laughter filled the room. They were laughing at themselves.

"You know," I continued, "you may think you guys are different from them and they may think they're different from you. But in many ways, you're not; and they're not. You're very much alike. I just want you to know that."

Alden and Mary's alternative high school is a community of at-risk, attention deprived students. It is also a community of creatively expressive and eloquent pupils. In fact, that describes every teenager I have ever met. But where the mainstream educational institution nurtures the ordinariness of growing up just like everyone else, this institution celebrates the wounds on the faces of its students which many other schools unfortunately overlook, mask or actively reconstruct.

As I walk through the hallways and notice teenagers with pierced lower lips, thick black eyeliner and multi-colored hair, I wonder how effective it is to shelter all these students from the mainstream. I am told they are here because "they will not survive out there. Here they can get the special attention they need." For some, this is their last chance.

Though I am struck by their irrepressible buoyancy, I am concerned for their future. Do they support one another in finding their own unique ways as they grow in the world, or do they incite each other to pick at the communal wound they seem to be trying to heal?

Towards the end of the day, I am invited to sit in on a health class subtitled, "What's Love Got To Do With It?" I listen as the students discuss their homework assignment: "What do I think my parents worry most about me?" Unanimously, they assume their parents' concerns: "That I won't make it to graduation... That I won't be able to survive without joining a gang... That I'll get involved with drugs."

Damien, who asks me to call him Digg, tells the class he is saving himself until he gets married. "I'm not having sex until my wedding night," he proudly declares.

"And you keep expecting us to believe that, Damien?" asks the room. "Why not? Just cause I act like a player? Is that why you don't believe me?" Digg sits back down in his seat, fixes the cap on his head and glances backwards to smile at me. I wink back, letting him know I believe him even if the class does not. Digg smiles at me again.

Though their ages vary, they seem tougher and older than some of the other teens I have met. Yet they encourage me to read them a story, an excerpt from a book I cherished as a teenager, *The Heart is a Lonely Hunter.* As I read about Mick Kelly and her high school crush on Harry and the time they went skinny dipping, I look around the room at these teenagers. These misfits of the mainstream. These lonely hunters. Staring back at me, they are lulled into a kind of sweet equanimity beneath the cadence of my soliloquy. I wonder if, when I was their age, had I gone to a school like this, I would be a different person. I am struck by the unmistakable beckoning for safety. I am grateful to have met Alden, Mary and the others.

But above all things, hanging out on Hope Street, I know that they are grateful to have found each other. ♛

Dear Scott,

I was having a conversation with a friend about life. At the end of our conversation, I asked her what she thought happened to us when we died and how we know if the way we live our life is the right way. She told me, "I don't know. And perhaps not knowing is part of life."

My family is originally from Brazil and twelve years ago, my mom, dad, sister and I came to the USA. Since my parent's separation and my father's moving out, the three of us grew closer than just mother and daughters (if that's possible). Then after fighting cancer for eight months, my mom, who was my best friend, my companion, my world, passed away, a week before Mother's Day. When she died, I didn't want to commit suicide and leave my sister alone. So, I thought that the best way was to talk her into suicide with me. Since I was already attending college and she had to continue with her school and work in order to support our financial status, we mostly kept in touch over the phone. I believe that the reason I never talked to her about committing suicide was because we didn't have the chance to spend so much alone time together. Whenever I went home for the weekend, there were always my mom's friends coming over to the house to see how we were doing. Also, school kept me busy.

Since my mom's death, my sister and I have struggled a lot. Life has shown us how cruel it can be. Despite everything that has happened, I still pray every night and I talk to my mom. I would do anything just to hear her voice one more time. Oh, how I miss her so!

I am usually a very friendly, smiley person. I'm one of those who always looks for the good in every bad and my friends know me as such. Until this day I have not wept in front of any of my friends because I feel that I should have to apologize if I did. I don't want them to see me that way. My dad ran to my arms every time he went to visit my mom in the hospital; I couldn't even depend on him. My mom was the one whose arms I ran to when I needed someone. Being the older one, I believe I have to be strong for my sister. Who can I run to? I believe we all have our own life to live and my life has not been any harder than the next person's. But just sometimes, when I am alone, hiding my tears from the world, I can't help but ask myself: "Why has this happened to me?"

— Eileen, age 19

What is death?
Death is just the end of a day
  Life begins again tomorrow
Death is my teacher
  Helping me to grow
Death is my biggest fear
  A shadow over my life
Death is a mystery
  Four friends together looking for the answer to a question
that doesn't exist

— Eli, Lauren, Max and Emily, age 16

8 | grieving death

Once there was a man taking a continuing education course entitled, "Life Without Grief." One day, when the teacher called in sick, there was a sign on the door to the classroom that read,

"Life Without Grief Will Be Canceled Today."

Every so often I will have lunch with a mother who has lost her son or daughter to AIDS. It is something I do for my friends who have died - taking care of their parents in a small way; reminding them who their children were in the world; telling them what important things they may never have known about their sons and daughters.

The mothers sit across the table, lean in towards me and put their hands on top of mine as they watch me chew my food. It is as if they are somehow nourished by seeing me eat, savoring the reflection, indirectly feeding their own child one last time. As they look into my eyes, we offer up our memories and we make each other cry. With tears as fresh as they were at the funerals, they prove to me that I, too, will not be forgotten.

"Bobby's father and I finally bought the boat we'd been saving up for," Barbara shared, "and we're calling it, 'Bobby's Dream.' He was my special one. My special one." She told me that none of his friends call anymore. "I wish they would, so I can say to them, 'Tell me about Bobby!' I need to know who he was."

One said to me, almost apologetically, "I shouldn't be talking so much about him anymore. I shouldn't be crying." When I asked why, she explained that her pastor, husband and other children all say, "It has been so many years; its enough already with the tears."

Another said, "We were a step upon his destiny. We rode with him to Glory."

Then they feed me with pictures of the grandchildren, the nieces and the nephews, the babies named for their sons and daughters. Their faces light up and there is joy at the table, alongside of the sorrow. In the very same conversation, in the very same sentence, they portray the ways in which they have made room for their worn-in grief alongside of their nascent gladness.

The mothers sit across the table from me. They show me their tears and they show me their joys. They have made room for both. And though many cannot see and feel what they see and feel, they have built their grief into an invisible kingdom and have inspired me with their courage to dwell there.

I prefer to think that the people I know who have died are saving me a place in line, that I'll finally get there and we can all be seated: "Thank you, the party is complete." I know there will be mourning, but I should like my years to be celebrated as well. I have loved my family and friends deeply. I had a rich, diverse, free life and I hope the energy of gratitude, aspiration and repose transcends my mortal existence and extends to those living in the universe and beyond.
– Michael Mitchell, 1962-1994

The infinity of loss. How does one begin the process of finding peace with such a faithful ache?

The process of grieving is one of staying in your body and discovering how you feel in the moment. Give yourself permission to have your feelings. Give yourself permission to spill your tears. Give yourself the time you need to be confused and angry. Sit down at your desk in front of your keyboard and begin to write. Get down on the floor and weep until you wish you could disappear into the very fiber of the carpet. Know that there is a very important difference between not wanting to be alive with these feelings, and wanting to die. Give yourself permission to feel both. Then remember that life is worth living.

Let the waves of heartache wash over you until you are drowning in your grief,
whatever its origin or cause. Make room for this experience in your interior world. This is a part of your life now. Know that one day you will

no longer see yourself as a sad person, but as someone who has known sadness. Though it seems that few, if any, can understand your sorrow, it exists still. It is your private refuge. Your solemn asylum. Have mercy on yourself as you would have on others.

In the beginning, loss forces the psyche to engage an inner emergency back-up system. A steady rush of adrenaline launches you far above the world of ordinary things as you evolve into a machine, able to perform human tasks never before imaginable. One of my teachers says, "A soldier never bleeds on the battlefield." Indeed, in the very beginning and for many ensuing months, you become an indwelling infantryman, ever alert and always on guard, protecting the boundaries of your psyche and the seat of your emotional faculties. And like any soldier, if you express too much discontent, the challenges are compounded.

Memories assault. Words distract. Comfort eludes.

The monarchy of grief is still miles away. Give your mind time to travel into your heart. Give your heart time to catch up to your body. Give your body time to reach home. In time, your sorrowing will begin. In shelter, your tears will find you.

Grief makes distant the once-in-reach horizon. It limits your visibility. It strands you in time. Grief inhibits your ability to move about freely inside your own life and leaves you lost, entirely locked inside your loved one's past. Grief enslaves you within a kingdom of invisibility. At certain times, you may be flooded with words that almost adequately describe your feelings. Most times, however, you may not be able to explain what it truly feels like, even to yourself.

Be gentle with yourself; you are standing under a different sky. Be careful with others; they may not understand. The well-intentioned words of comfort from friends and companions may have a tendency to ensnare you even deeper inside your sense of aloneness. Sometimes a common-place but heartfelt expression like, "How are you?" can sound cliche and tediously unoriginal to the mourner. "If you have to ask," you might hear yourself thinking, "then my grief truly has diminished me."

I remember my first experience visiting the Names Project AIDS

Memorial Quilt. Forty-five thousand panels representing only a small percentage of those we have lost. Laid out on the National Mall in the Capital, the offerings from faithful hearts. The mile-long stretch of grief and lost glory. The shrine for the stillborn dawning of an unforgotten life. Yet, shrouded in that union of mass sorrow, I felt somewhat more alone in my own.

Who am I among the millions of others?

Who am I amidst the church of memory? Who am I amongst the living, the grieving, those left behind? If, with a collective sorrow, we walk the corners of the cloth, who will understand my own private pain?

There may be friends and family members who will not be able to listen. Some people are allergic to other people's sorrow. Be careful how you share your sadness in this time. Surround yourself with people who love you, adore you and see you the way that you want to be seen.

Seek out places to be witnessed and validated, received and remembered.

In Judaism, the mourner is required to recite a specific prayer three times a day for an entire year in the presence of nine other Jews. Though they may be complete strangers, standing behind the mourner, listening to the "Kaddish," written in both Hebrew and Aramaic, the congregants unite into a chorus of truth, an assembly of acknowledgment. They are the ultimate witnesses, regarding with great respect the mourner's process, giving testimony to an ineffable sorrow. With the final Amen, they venerate the burden of death. It is as if they are saying, "I hear you. I notice the mark that grief has made. I will remember and hold your place among the living while you honor his place among the dead."

"I've got your back."

A mother of a high school student in California writes:

This has been a year of extraordinary loss for my family. In thirteen months, our circle was reduced by nine lives. Each death was painful, only one was "chronologically correct," whatever that means. Expanding to include the sadness, allowing for the anger and the tears, the joy and the gratitude, the inconsolable loneliness was, and continues to be a demanding journey. There were very few friends or family members who could hold the space for our grief. There was no road map for the emotional terrain we each had to cover.

The process required a profound growing of wisdom: forgiveness for the impatient; gentleness for the intolerant; kindness for the insensitive. Stillness. Yes, so much stillness as the storms raged and raged. More than anything, each of us has had to learn to be tender with our own rawness and respectful of our individual process, whatever form that takes on any given day. Over and over, again and again.

Here is a list of inappropriate things to say to a mourner:

How are you?

I know exactly how you feel

We've all been there

Besides that news, how's everything else in your life?

He's in a better place now

It gets better with time

It's time to move on

Do you think you'll ever be happy again?

Time heals all pain

When will the old "you" be back?

Let me tell you about how I dealt with it when it happened to me...

He wouldn't want you to be this way

Call me

Remember him how he was

I can't tell you what or how to feel – but...

God only gives us as much as we can handle

Heaven needed another angel

He was picked because he was special

It never gets better. Trust me. I've been there. I know.

What doesn't kill us, makes us stronger

Things only happen for the best

I'm concerned you're becoming unglued

You should only know good things from now on

One of my teachers used to say, "Sometimes when we give over to it, we have to stop and wait for things to gather in. Let the mind and body heal it." How long should it take to get over a loss? As long as it takes. And then a little bit longer. The more important question is: how much compassion can you have for yourself during the whole process?

I think that most people can't, or don't want to put into words their feelings and experiences of death. Because we expect a lack of communication in experiences with death, love and loneliness we are afraid to ask, for fear of offending someone or putting them in an 'uncomfortable' position. But although people may be hesitant at first, I think we need to talk about these things to each other, and maybe we need the prompt of someone asking us specifically how we felt, or details about our experience.
—Ruth, age 18

Here is a list of appropriate things to say that will help the mourner:

I care
I see you
I'm always thinking of you
Your sorrow matters
I am so sorry for your loss
I can tell that you are in pain
I see what this has done to you
Tell me the last thing you said to each other
Tell me about the things he loved in life
Tell me what he called you
I have faith in your ability to handle this
Take all the time you need
No need for words to or for me
Be who you need to be
Tonight I am tasting the salt of your tears; even the ones that you aren't able to cry yet
Let my thoughts of you keep you company through this time
I will hold onto your dreams while you deal with this reality
Please know that your grief has not diminished you

Jillian is a teenager who lost her best friend in a car accident. "I should be able to see her when she's thirty and have lunch and drink coffee and talk about the past. And then not see her for another ten years. But now I can never do that. We were a pair," she told me. "If she could die then anyone can, including me." The insufferable acceptance. The emptying of hands. The "what now?" of life. The wishing they were out there somewhere in the world, having dinner, watching a football game, making new friends, moving closer to the realization of their every dream. In his coming to terms with death, one teen wrote, "It's not the end. I will call it simply, the stopping point."

As we walk through life, our losses walk with us.
Yet, the many devoted friendships and other relationships that have changed in such dramatic ways certainly stay with us, as well. As one teen says, "His love is still with me." They are ever with us, our loved ones, moving and inspiring us, settling into places inside of us which others may never reach, perhaps even helping us to learn the lessons in life we would have learned were they still here to teach us.

After the death of my mother to breast cancer, the framework of parental support I had relied upon after all those years could never be put back together again in the same formation. I would have to find a way to create new support, to turn my greatest weakness into strength. I needed to get back to living again rather than focusing on the part of me that died. "Take control, claim it for your own and figure out how to move on." I was sure that I heard that message from my mother, late at night when I lay in bed thinking about her.
– Andie, age 17

In the Jewish tradition there is a saying: Whenever a person walks down the street he is preceded by a host of angels crying, "Make way! Make way for the Image of God." It comes from one of the central concepts of Judaism, the expression, "B'tzelem Elohim." Translated to English it means that each human being is created with and depicts Divine worth. As a boy in hebrew school, I always wondered what part of me portrayed God's Image? How did my divinity express itself? Was it in skill, success or perfection? Was it in action, good deeds or purity? Where inside of me was God's likeness?

Many years later, at the funeral for my Aunt Lil, I got my answer. Only a few months before his fiftieth wedding anniversary, my Uncle Seymour was now standing beside his wife's coffin. Hunched under the weight of grief, already thickly settled, his shoulders sank with each exhalation. Emptied of self, he held out his hands and surrendered to sorrow. Gone was his distinctive flair and style. His penetrating laugh. His heart. Yet in their absence was a radiant realness, an accessibility to something soft and authentic. Never before had I witnessed such vulnerability. Such humility. God's Image.

Grieving is our connection to the world.

It gets us in touch with our shared humanity and delivers us back to the beginning, where there was perfection. Grief is not the emanation of all things Divine; but in its presence, it reveals that which is most holy in all of us. A reflection of genuineness. A refraction of hope. A ripening of love.

At the end of Lil's eulogy, my uncle read aloud the secret words they shared to express their esteemed union: "With a love that knows no limits, no bounds, and is as never ending as infinity."

On the day of my father's funeral, I looked at the files in the left-hand side drawer of his desk, as he had instructed. In the very back, held together by a paper clip, were a stack of index cards, typewritten notes on how to comfort the mourner. On the first card, in his own handwriting, were these words:

"Even in times of sorrow the mourner must remember all that is good and worth living for, for God has created a basically good and lovable world. In the years that you are privileged to share, your life must bring many pleasures and teach much by your example. And your remains will lie not only in this plot of ground, but in every heart your life will touch."

I want to tell the world all
about my friend and have them listen.
I don't see him as the boy who died of a disease.
I see him as Keith, the boy who bleached his wavy hair
that curled around his ears. Keith, who always wore
khakis and cracked me up. Keith, who will always be
with me no matter what happens.

In summer, I go on vacation to the mountains with
my family. We stay in a house on a lake. It is the most
beautiful place in the world. When I was there this past
summer, I went out onto the dock one night and talked
to the stars, because I think Keith is a part of the stars.

Keith iS the stars.

I can look up at them and know he's in them, and
he always will be. The stars will keep burning and
he will stay a part of them and in that way,
I'll be able to see him whenever I want.

— Tiffany, age 16

John Fletcher Harris

"Good morning" whispers a smiling black nurse in a pink uniform. "I'm so busy, I didn't even say hello to you."

"That's okay," I hear myself saying over the classical music playing on the transistor radio. "I'm not really all here myself."

I am sitting in St. Vincent's Hospital in room #536 with my friend John Fletcher Harris who is dying. Looking over at him, he seems so much like many other of my friends who have journeyed here before. Unconscious, with eyes half-open and rolled back into his head, he is stealing fast and short breaths, yet also quite heavy and loud ones. He inhales through his mouth while a clear tube streams air into his nostrils.
A single tear extends down the left side his face as his body groans from the effort of breathing.

Each nurse who appears enters in silence, with respect for the room, as they perform their quarter-hour check-up. They share with me their readiness for his death yet allow me to express something of myself. "How are you feeling today?" or "Are you a relative?" they ask. A red-haired nurse with patient eyes tells me, "We'll be coming back if you need us for anything," and leaves me to be alone with my friend.

As I sit I notice how tight my chest has become and how much breath is trapped inside of me, as if it were an insult to exhale. So I begin matching John's breathing, three fast but deep inhalations. A stuffed animal tucked under the sheet leaning in towards his heart reads, "Frontier Bear." I am with my friend and I don't want to say goodbye.

Minutes later, an older man in a well-tailored suit introduces himself to me as John's doctor and motions me to meet with him outside the room. "I don't know if you're aware but John's very close to dying and we're here to help him if he's in any pain. But he doesn't seem to be at the moment." After a pause he asks, "Did you know?"

"I've been out of town," I answer, "but was told last night that I shouldn't be surprised if he's not here when I come to visit today."

"He probably has another twelve hours."

Taken by his openness I respond, "Thanks for telling me. That's really kind of you." "Well," he smiles, "you're here." Then he walks away.

I return to my friend and awkwardly whisper, "John, it's Scott. I've come to visit with you. I don't know if you can hear me but if you can, I just came to say that I love you and I'm going to sit here for a little while."

And I sit and wait. I sit and watch. I sit and remember the night, only months earlier, when after leading one of his prayer circles he reached out to hug me but picked me up over his head instead and paraded me around the room. I remember the times I would rush home after those prayer circles in order to write down into my journal all the poetic things he would say. And I remember the first time a woman named Nora came to the prayer circle. She was weeping in the dark, in the back of the room, when John interrupted himself to say, "I can't continue while someone here is in pain; I have to help. What is it?"

"When I release something," she began, "I wish it would stop coming back." At once we all knew she was referring to her cancer. So with his suggestion we drew her into the center of the room and enclosed ourselves around her, some of us embracing her, others lightly touching a hand or a leg.

John's groans become louder and longer. As the bed shakes with each exhalation, "Frontier Bear" moves a bit. Two nurses peek their heads into the doorway; they notice that I am still here. How long should I stay? Does he want to die with me in the room? Should anyone die alone?

I reach for the journal in my knapsack, the journal with John's poetry, and I prepare myself to read out loud. I walk over to the side of the bed closest to his ear, feeling silly, wondering if he will recognize his words.

"John. It's Scott... I'm gonna go now, but I want to tell you something you told me last year. It's some of your poetry. And I want you to hear it now."

I begin to read in between the quick and heavy inhalations, in between the groans, in between the sounds of the machine inducing oxygen into his lungs. Carefully and slowly I read so that he can hear me, if it is at all possible. And it suddenly seems to me that he can. Even though his breathing is as loud as ever, it seems his attention is on listening. I read with growing confidence, over the noise of decay, knowing no matter how softly I speak, he is with me.

> *Stand up*
> *Let your leaves fall all around you*
> *And with bare branches*
> *Expose yourself to the sun*
> *Expose yourself to God*

The following Monday at John's prayer circle, we passed around his favorite talking stick and shared our favorite stories. Julio, through many tears said that he loved John very much, "And I told him so."

Iver recited an Indian Poem:

> *God to the right of me*
> *God to the left of me*
> *Above and below*
> *Behind and in front*
> *And God within me*

Don shared a eulogy he had written, closing with the words:

> *There is no end*

Finally, Philip floated into the room donning huge angel wings made of white diaphanous netting and gossamer feathers attached to his shoulders, trailing down to the floor. Standing in the middle of our circle he talked about John's silence, how he would pause in between sentences or even in the middle of a thought, sometimes for a minute, sometimes even longer. "Never before had someone been

able to make me feel how valuable silence can be."
Then, lifting his arms so that his wings created a canopy
above us, he recited one of John's poems.

> *Sometimes my feathers are a little awry*
> *And sometimes my life is a bit of a lie*
> *But still I fly*
> > *Still I fly*

Dear Scott,

My name is Lilly. I am sixteen and I think I'm well
on my way to "doing a whole bunch of stuff,"
as my brother once put it. I have traveled the country,
worked at a school in the Ukraine and once found
the bathroom by myself in Paris. I think that
the Curious George store in Harvard Square is almost
as good as Starbucks and I intend to live for
a long time. I've always liked the idea of one hundred
and twenty years. I believe the soul learns to speak at
different times for each person, no matter how long
they have been on earth.

I think, I ponder. I suppose. I wonder.

Am I forgetting to do something? Am I missing out on
some aspect of teenage-dom that is so vital to the rest of
my life? Have I left something out? Or someone? I want
to do it all. My friend says, "Oh, there is so much

I want to do. I could never get it done." I tell him, "Start now! What are you waiting for?"

If only I could make sure that there was a way to do everything I've always wanted, like hang-gliding or piercing my left ear (I'm keeping my right ear with only one, but the left has three) or learning to make flowers with icing or how to successfully download material online or even things I can't yet fathom that I will someday want to do. If only I could hold some magical machine in my hand that could bring back the morning to make sure I told my brother how proud I am of him or tell my friends how much they mean to me and how deeply in debt I am to my parents for all they have given me. But I don't. The best I can do is choose life and speak my truth.

My name is Lilly. I am sixteen and I know I can't do it all. But I think I'm well on my way to "doing a whole bunch of stuff."

— Lilly, age 16

"...while we all have our different living circumstances, it's so vital to find ourselves in a space of pure love where our tears, our thoughts, our encouragements are all accepted... where joy is brought into our lives and where we are taught to observe and hold our own pain... where selflessness and compassion are brought out in all of us. I see not one person who is not a precious piece of glory... may I always see into people as I do right now."

    –Zohar, age 19

9 | choosing life

One weekend I was asked to lead some sessions with a group of high school seniors from Atlanta who had traveled to Florida by bus. The theme for the weekend was "Choosing Life." Their advisor gave me the freedom to go anywhere I wanted with the subject, so I decided to use the story of my friend Edgardo.

Edgardo, who died in 1990, was fighting the AIDS virus for years when he decided to no longer choose life. On a late January afternoon, not long after making it through his final Christmas, he very consciously and courageously asked to be removed from all life-sustaining medicine and support. Requesting that only the morphine be kept dripping through his veins in order to reduce or remove any pain and discomfort that would set in, he prepared to die as morning approached.

As I told his story, the teens sat still, absorbing every single word. It brought me back to my days fresh out of high school working as a camp counselor for a group of six year-old boys, "The Cadets." Back then, I quickly learned that the best way to keep a small child's attention at story-time was to use the word "cemetery" or "funeral" every so often. It worked every time, especially when a vampire would pay an occasional visit to a graveyard. I think it is our fascination with mortality at any age that keeps us attended to the present moment and forces us to look more carefully at the road before us. I told the Atlanta teens how I arrived at Gardo's hospital room late in the evening and sat with him through the night, with his sister Iliana kneeling on the floor on the other side of the bed. Keeping vigil with my friend, his sister and I reminisced about his life and our relationship to him; about his first time doing drag on Halloween a few years back when he found a pair of black high-heeled pumps in a men's size eleven. And how old he was.

"Thirty-four," I said.

"No, no. He is definitely thirty-five," Iliana whispered. "I would know, he's my little brother."

Out of the silence, with his head turned towards the window Edgardo suddenly muttered, "I'm thirty-five." He was still with us, just lying there, staying awake and listening to us as long as he could, until the break of dawn.

"Go home," Gardo told me. "It's late. I can't believe that you're still here."

"I can't," I whispered, quite dramatically. "I don't want to leave you. This is the most beautiful place in the entire world tonight." I told the teens how he turned his head towards me and with a weak stare that could not belie his irresistible cynicism, said, **"Oh Scott. Get a life!"**

In choosing this conscious cadence towards death, on this special night-watch, Edgardo taught me how to fully choose life. The opposite of "choosing life" is to "choose to not live an authentic life," even in the final moments before death.

I have been diagnosed with depression since 8th grade but I was depressed long before then. I just never felt like I was important or special. I am constantly crying and I'm not motivated. I want to be perfect but I'm not. I have tried to kill myself three times and have been in a hospital once. All in all, I don't want to live. I feel so stupid telling you all of this. Here I am with such stupid problems and you probably just can't understand why I don't value life. I guess it's because I don't feel I have a good one.
– LaRonna, age 17

No teenager's problems are ever "stupid."
Your experiences, fears and bouts of depression are as important to the world as anyone else's. You exist and you are valuable. Your feelings matter. In fact, your story is part of the larger story. Your experiences and feelings help sensitize and deepen the world around you. When you have the strength to be vulnerable, you teach the world how to be vulnerable. **Hurt is a minefield that blows you wide open and gives you the ability to help navigate others through their mines.** I once told a crying teenage girl, "It gets better." She responded with, "No it doesn't." I may not have been able to convince her, but you can. As you go along in life, you can demonstrate for others a positive model of survival. Growing up is not as harsh as it may sometimes seem because there are other people like you in the world who make it easier.

*I've been realizing lately how much our lives are out of our control.
We have guidance counselors in school telling us where to go to college.
We have reckless drivers who may kill us in an instant. There are terrorists
who just want to hurt us because we live in a different country. Sometimes
I feel like my future is being altered without my consent. My friend once
said that when he is upset he just thinks about how insignificant he is in
the universe. He's really smart and I usually agree with him, but this time
I don't. I think we are all so important in the universe. There are bugs
in the ground that feel the earth shake when I walk across my lawn.
There is a tree that breathes in the carbon dioxide that I breathe out.
There is a person out there that I waved on in my car when there was
heavy traffic and he needed to turn. I affect all these beings. I am important.
– Liz, age 16*

Nineteen year-old Abigail from New York tells me, **"Yield to your brilliance, even when it hurts."** I know the feelings of being depressed and confused, scared and alone. And of even not wanting to be alive. Before you can come to terms with the feelings of specialness inside, sometimes you have to feel the ugliness as well. The agony. The sorrow. Know that even in those moments, you are blessed - not only when you have enthusiasm for life, but in the darkened times as well. In that way you can start to see that you are worthy and valuable, even in your sorrow. Your confidence is not what makes you holy. Having a boyfriend or girlfriend is not what makes you valuable. Getting into the school of your dreams is not the measure of true success. The healing happens when you become acquainted with the stuff on the inside and when you sit in the confusion - when you ache and when you cry - as well as when you laugh and when you joke. When you are the most honest you can be with yourself. The quietest. The emptiest. That is your value and your success. Because that is your strength. And that is where things of true power can access you. Think about it.

*I think, like many teenagers, I always questioned the "beauty and
innocence" of youth. I never possessed the patience or conviction in the
process of growing up and coming of age. However, in being confronted
with my friend's death, I found myself blatantly staring at my disillusionment
and ignorance. For at age nineteen, he left a world which elicits
so many questions of myself. Love, friendship, success and even failure*

I now more than ever anxiously await to experience. His passing has made me aware of the reality of life's fragility as well as the vulnerability we all share, simply by being human.
– Jill, age 19

My friend Dominick, after being diagnosed with cancer said, "The cancer didn't make me big; the cancer made me see how big I already was!" You are on a journey of self-discovery. Salute yourself for all the tears you cry and for all the hours of deep and meaningful introspection ahead. Instead of saying, "I hate my life," try saying, "I hate my life today." In that way, you keep open the option of changing your mind tomorrow.

Listen to your thoughts and learn to love the inner

process that is unfolding. You have the stuff of heroes in there, but you must believe that. You must believe that it is worth it to stay alive - that it is possible to live with confusion. This is still a good life, even with some of the pain. You must believe that. I do. A student once handed me a letter about her brother who got infected with HIV at the age of fourteen. On his gravestone were etched the words, "Be careful with your life for it is the only one you have." I am glad I never killed myself after I got the news about my HIV and after the many funerals of my friends.

I am glad I stayed here.

Even if there is a time I can't be composed, I have friends who will be, and if they feel like falling apart I'll be the one standing straight.
And if we both lose our wits, I have a plan. We'll cry and cry and then we'll talk. And then we'll sing. As loud and as strong and as best as we can, we will sing. Who knows what makes the earth go 'round, but it is definitely singing that makes the blood keep flowing. Somewhere in the back of my brain, the part that is connected to my soul, I get it. I totally get it. One day I think I'll understand it enough to voice it out loud. Right now, there is only one thing I know for sure. Feeling like your life is over and wanting to let go or just quit is okay. The thing that isn't okay is giving in to that urge. Overrule the unfairness with love, compassion and a willingness to live.
– Alisa, age 17

As you remember compassion of self, know that you are enough.

Beyond all things, there is room in this world for your pain - and your joy.

As my friend Ruth always says, "there is room in this world for the things of beauty in you."

My father always tells me how proud he is of all my accomplishments, but I don't want him to believe that because I am afraid that if I fail at something I will hurt him and his pride for me would be shattered. The other day he called and said one of the nicest things anyone has ever said to me. He said he wanted to be me. He said, "Paul, you have so much to work with and you don't realize it yet. I wish that I could either be you with all that I now know or bestow all my knowledge on you." I realized then that I really do have a lot to work with and I could make more attempts to harness that energy but that it can only come through loving myself. Yet the fact that I am trying to love myself is an indirect way of saying that I already do, because I wouldn't give all this attention to it if I didn't really care for myself.
– Paul, age 16

At the end of the weekend retreat on "Choosing Life," we rode back home on the bus in the middle of the night. Our bellies were filled with fried dough and ice cream from the two amusement parks we visited and our muscles were exhausted from standing in long lines, riding on roller coasters and racing to buy more tickets to do it all again. Our hearts were full as well. There was a feeling of freedom to momentarily adore and appreciate the choice we made to choose life for another day. Before falling asleep against Emily's shoulder, Abe said,

"My life right now is the widest open door there is."

Those moments, at the threshold of morning, alone, amidst the calm clamor of a busload of teens, reminded me of my own mortality. Stolen moments before daybreak, with the burden of death over one shoulder and the burden of life over the other, rewarded me with promise. In the quiet company of the sleeping teens, I had settled upon the resting pulse of possibility.

Somewhere north of Orlando near the Georgia state line, I heard a tune and some lyrics coming from a song on the bus driver's radio. "Here's my shoulder, you can lean on me." It was dark. I was tucked into my seat, second from front on the right-hand side, my laptop wedged in between my knees and the gray glow from its screen lighting my tiny corner of the world. This, my silent sanctuary amid the muffled sounds of teens sleeping at the back of the bus. This, my protection from thoughts of the fleetingness of life, of the weeks ahead, with the daunting visits to my doctor's office. This, my distraction from the ritual of swallowing my HIV pills every day. I looked back and saw legs sprawled out into the aisle, faces pressed up against window panes and mouths hanging open. Huddled into my seat with the warmth of my flannel shirt wrapped around me, thoughts of the day were spinning within. Staying awake for as long as I could, I waited for morning as it fast approached on the long ride home.

To be brave is to be generous to our-selves in believing that, in the middle of the road that

twists and bends, wherever we are in the world, we matter. We all have a place in each others' lives, however brief or anonymous. Offer what love you can. We can all have an ingenuous way of holding the emptiness inside of another, however unending and profound. Give whatever you have. We all have arms that wish to hold onto the people in our lives, however firmly or unfixedly. Stitch your soul to their shadows. Like Edgardo, stay up a little longer into your private night and embrace the warmth of the company you keep.

One of the teens asked two final questions for the weekend. "Where's the line between curiosity and self-destructive behavior? How will I learn to behave responsibly and still live fully?"

I told Ben that every day when we awaken, we are given the chance to make a new choice. We get to renegotiate a contract we made with our-selves. We get to choose life each morning. And if the choices we made yesterday do not feel right today, we are given this new day to choose again. Choose a little more life in each early moment before morning.

On that special night-watch in Gardo's hospital room, his sister imparted her own wisdom. "Hold onto life, Scott. I don't care how you do it - through prayer and meditation or talking it out with someone - or like my brother did, dressing up in drag."

Whatever you do, just hold onto life.

The cloud of people who drift with me
The grass I sit on that rustles beneath
The warmth that splashes on my skin
The rivers of blood that rush inside
There are no words to say my prayer
I will write my prayer with my life
— Samson, age 16

The old Man at the gate

The young December chill wrapped itself around the rutted streets of the Old City. In the narrow alleyways of the Arab market it was a challenge just to move windward through the cold, past the creeping crowds of shoppers and vendors haggling over souvenirs and other trinkets. Jerusalem, that early winter, was business as usual. I stopped in front of an Arab man selling age-old artifacts and disposable cameras from his tiny hut, inviting me to bargain. Gently, he slapped his hand across my face and smiled. "I make a nice price for you," he said before inhaling deeply into the open end of the long rubber pipe on his houka. I shook my head and moved along, deflecting his appeals with a wave of my hand.

Into the crowd I disappeared and searched for Jason, one of my eighteen year-old students from Florida spending the year in an Israeli yeshiva. "It's their way of warming up to you," he would later tell me of that slap, still feeling the shape of the vendor's hand across my face. Swept away by the undertow of pedestrian traffic, I continued on and headed towards the Jaffa Gate where Jason would then meet me and escort me to the Western Wall.

The Wall, or Kotel as it is known in Hebrew, stands on the site of the First Temple that was destroyed when the walls of Jerusalem were breached by Nebuchadnezzar and the Babylonians in the year 586 BC. It is also the only remaining structure that surrounded the Second Temple when Jerusalem was once again destroyed, this time by Titus and the Romans, in the year 70 A.D, killing two and a half million people and exiling a million more.

Every day hundreds of people with hearts in hand and prayers in pocket stand before it, asking God to fix them or put them back together again. As it is written in the Book of Lamentations, "Renew our days as You have done as of old." Like soldiers of survival in a battle for an indwelling peace, they stand at attention before the Western Wall.
Like a hotline to heaven where tourists-turned-pilgrims call out their prayers, the Wailing Wall reflects all that is indestructible in the human spirit.

I met Jason at the top of an immense staircase leading down to a wide plaza of people shuffling about, mostly under their fur-trimmed black hats. "Right about here, on this step,"

he said, "This is usually the spot where I lower my voice."
We descended the stairs together.

"Why?" I asked. Glowing with anticipation, he placed his index finger against his lips, perpendicular to his half-smile and said, "Shhh..." Jason was lathering himself in the honor of teaching his teacher. "Look all around you. Prayers are rising."

As we approached the narrow gateway before the Wall, a beggarly old man held out a pair of tefillin, a type of wooden amulet that a Jew is commanded to wear during morning worship services. The long strands of leather attached to the two black boxes filled with scripture were as weathered and worn as the skin on the old man's face. As he mumbled something in what seemed like an antiquated mystical language, Jason reached into his pocket and tossed a few shekels into the old man's cup. "He said that you should be careful not let the headpiece of the tefillin touch the wall."

"Is that all?" I asked. "He seemed to be saying something else, but I couldn't quite make it out." Jason nodded his head in agreement and replied, "I think it was some kind of... prayer."

The weather warmed with each step we took towards the formidable stone structure. I removed my jacket and wrapped it around my waist. Jason watched carefully as I set one small black box of the tefillin against my right bicep and entwined the attached leather strap seven times around my arm, opposite my heart. Then I placed the other small box on my forehead letting two more straps of leather hang down either side of my torso. Together, we whispered the appropriate prayers. "Thus says the Lord: I will betroth you to me forever and I will betroth you to me with righteousness, with love, with justice and with compassion." Finally, with the remaining quarter yard of strap hanging from my wrist, I wrapped my hand in leather, winding it three times around my fingers, three more times over my hand, and tethering the rest around and into my palm.

Standing on my left was a young soldier in an olive colored uniform with his M16 rifle resting vertically at his side. Eyes closed and prayer book open, his body swayed right, then left. He bent his knees and bowed his shoulders before the wall of peace. Standing on my right was a Hasidic man in a long black coat and curled sideburns underneath his wide-brimmed hat.

Eyes closed and prayer book open, his body swayed left, then right. He rocked his head back and forth and moved his lips in syncopation to the words in his heart, before the wall of supplication. As I stood there, open-eyed, empty-handed and with no book to guide me I realized that people pray in passionate ways. Although we look and behave differently from one another, when the sun is on our backs and we stand before the future we all seem to burn with a similar fire.

As a child I was taught, "Just as a man flails his arms above the water when he is drowning, so does a man shake when he prays." Bowing my head, studying the ground at my feet, I understood that I too had come to drown before the wall of worship. Flanking my shoes were puddles of carefully folded white paper pieces, the overflow of handwritten appeals beseechingly inserted in between the narrow cracks of Jerusalem stone. Prayers on paper beweeping the story of a life, one after the other after the other. With the excess freight of longing lying at my feet, I began to consider my own prayer. Not having written anything down as evidence, as offering to place within the crevices before me, I wondered if this ancient altar of stone would be able to read the words languishing in my heart. I leaned my head against the Wall and tears settled into the corners of my eyes. With the small black box of scripture resting against my forehead scraping the stone, I closed my eyes, dug my fingers into an ancient incision and began to pray.

Adonai, Hineni

Dear God, here I am

Searching my mind for any remnant of a blessing memorized from childhood, I listened for my father's voice leading Saturday morning services on holidays in synagogue, and my Uncle Seymour's annual soliloquy as he led our family Passover seders, or any other bittersweet emotional intrusion. I had come to ask God to take away my HIV. To not allow me to die of AIDS. To forbid the world to ever forget my name. "Not me. Please not me. Don't make me into yet another piece of cloth on the Memorial Quilt, brilliantly laid out on a sparkling morning for all to see. Don't celebrate the song of my soul with a candle in the night amidst thousands of others. Don't honor me with silence." I searched for the right sequence of syllables, a conse-crated sentence that would give the proper heft to my plea. Yet all I could locate was one word:

Thanks

Thanks

> *For the sun on my back*
> *For the pulsing of life in my veins*
> *And for the T-cells in my blood*

Thanks

> *For the soldier on my left and the Hasid on my right*
> *For Jason standing by*
> *And for the old man at the gate*

Thanks

> *For the plane that will take me home*
> *For the faces that will smile with greetings*
> *And for friends I have yet to meet with eyes that laugh*
>   *and arms that hold*

> *Here is my simple prayer of gratitude for*
> *the very breath of life in me*
> *Thank you for all this and more*

> *PS...Please help me to remember my prayer when I need it most*

Dear Scott,

I was talking to my friend one day and she kept trying to
tell me how confident and strong I am. "Take boys, Claudia,"
she said. "When it doesn't work out for me and a guy
I blame it on him. I call him an asshole. I will do whatever
I need to bolster my threatened self-esteem, even if it's distorting
the simple truth that someone doesn't want to be with me.
You on the other hand say, 'Well, he doesn't want to be with
me and I think he should, because i AM iNTERESTiNG.
But he doesn't and that sucks, and that's the end of it.'
It's great that you can be that comfortable with yourself."

I like what my friend said about me. It made me feel strong
and I like to feel strong and in control. But I'm not always
in control of my emotions. And I almost told myself
I wasn't worth a whole lot last night.

I liked the looks of this boy, Bryan. He was sort of quirky
and a little bit of a mystery. I like to analyze people and
I hadn't "pegged" him. So I had this hope that there was
something really worth getting to know even though I hadn't
seen it yet. Bottom line, I was very attracted to him and
that attraction skewed my realistic way of thinking.

We hooked up pretty immediately when we were in
the same room. There wasn't a lot of talking.
This happened twice more and I think he was

finally bored, because he said, "I really want to have sex with you." And I just let it hang in the air. For a second, my rules about sex became relative. I told myself it wasn't a huge deal. It was scary how suddenly everything became relative. I actually felt a little guilty because he had done more sexually for me than I had for him.

I was lying there actually considering what to do when it struck me! We only had a few conversations and every opportunity that I had given him to know more about me, BECAUSE i AM iNTERESTiNG, had been ignored. And every opportunity I had given him to tell me about himself had been ignored. I realized then that he wasn't that interesting. I realized that he did not care at all, AT ALL, about getting to know me. So I said, "Thank you, but no."

I remember how valuable I felt that day. I think I remember I felt sacred that day. We have to hold to an absolute and holy definition of sacredness. I think we have to remember its absoluteness when moments like this one devalue our sense of self, and threaten to make everything relative and erase our interestingness.

I am Claudia and i AM iNTERESTiNG.

— Claudia, age 16

I am, have been and always will be sacred. I have to embrace that. I live by the truth and move onto the next step. Moving onto the next step can be just as scary. Scarier than the truth. What else can I do but be as honest as I know?

Demanding a miracle is a scary thing. I keep thinking I might be taking away someone else's miracle. That there is only so much Divine matter in the universe to go around, and there must be somebody, somewhere out there who is more beautiful than me. So I settle for what comes. And if it should hurt, am I still sacred?

— Trevor, age 19

10 | sacredness

"You gave my friend Leslie advice about her boyfriend Jared, who broke up with her after seven months. I was wondering if you would be able to give me some advice also." Anthony approached me one day searching for answers. "There's this girl I've liked ever since I first saw her in eighth grade," he began. "At the time, I wanted to tell her how I felt but I was afraid she didn't feel the same way about me."

As I listened to him, I remembered my own high school crushes and unrequited longings. "Let me guess," I interjected. "If you're anything like I was, then you've fantasized, waited, thought about asking but were afraid of rejection, fantasized some more, waited some more and then wondered if it's better to just be friends. Sound familiar?"

"Pretty much exactly!" he responded. "I was going to tell her in ninth grade and also in tenth. Now I'm a junior and I have the same feelings. We've become good friends but I'm still contemplating whether to pursue this or just let it go. I have the Junior Prom later this year and I want to ask her to go with me."

I wondered if, in his quest to win her affection, Anthony had neglected to notice all the other really great girls who undoubtedly wanted to get to know him. If all he was seeing was what he thought he could never have, was his marginalized focus making him feel even more inferior and lonely? Had she even earned all this attention he was placing on her?

He continued sharing his thought process. "You wrote in your first book that teenagers give you their hope in return for a chance to be free from their fear. Well, my hope is that she will feel the same way towards me as I do towards her and my fear is that she'll turn me down."

I smiled at his dedication to this issue and searched for the words that would support his honor, for Anthony was about to set foot upon **the proving ground of adolescence: surviving rejection.** "Let me ask you this," I began, "do you have the courage to risk being vulnerable in front of her for the intent purpose of learning about yourself, your sacredness, regardless of her response?" I was hoping he would see that in contributing his honesty he would be revealing his true essence, not just to her, but more importantly, to himself.

"The fear that you talk about," I continued, "is what makes you appealing; it's what makes you accessible, a person who somebody wants. It makes you a the kind of guy that someone else deserves." I was trying to get him to understand all that he has to offer, beyond mere looks and personality: his naivete, his unknowingness, his beginningness. "Your fear is your value; it gives you substance. See it that way if you can. Honor that part of you. I've had many crushes," I added. "Once, I even got up the guts to ask one out. He answered with, 'I'm on the fly' and it took me a while to translate that as a 'no.' But I learned so much. Sure it didn't turn out the way I planned, but I got more out of it than I expected."

"What do you mean?" Anthony asked.

"I mean that I learned how to risk being vulnerable in front of another person. I mean that I stood there, feeling unfamiliar and awkward, and said words like "um" and "so" and even nothing at all. I mean that I learned how, for just a second, to drop my hands and my defenses and with no tricks up my sleeves, let someone else see me - the real me; the tender me; the side closest to the raw, sweet, wanting and confused part of me. And in having someone really see this more truthful version of myself, I experienced the depth of my desire and source of my sacredness, and I loved myself for it."

"I am not a virgin, and I know that even though I've had those one-hour relationships, I will never give my body to anyone I don't love ever again." Laura, eighteen years-old, was sitting on her knees, squeezed into the corner of a misshaped circle of students in a youth group lounge. "I know that a teenager could be in a one-hour relationship and still hurt more than if it was for like eight months." She described her experience with a guy who said he loved her, "But I don't think he really meant it." Instead of fully revealing herself, she used the pronoun 'you' in place of 'I.' "You think you are in love with someone and then you realize you were in something alone and you wonder if you can ever get your sacredness back." She taught the room about one of the reasons a person decides to be, what she calls, a 'born-again virgin.' "It's both difficult and empowering. You feel a sense of possession over yourself," she said. "You always know your boundaries and there's no confusion about how far to go." She admitted that it allayed her anxieties and helped her become more acquainted with an unmet or lost feeling of sanctity. "Sometimes you just don't ever want to hurt again."

One of the most persuasive letters I've ever received comes from a college student in Delaware. Written in blue ink and script, Meredith's words seem to resonate with many of my students and have stimulated numerous responses.

I have never really had a boyfriend, not that I have not wanted one.
I am 21 years-old and have been on maybe five dates. I am looking
but most of the time I end up being "one of the guys." And up until now
that has been fine. I was the girl that guys came to for advice about
what to get their girlfriend, how to ask a girl out or how to break up
with a girl. When I think about sex my hormones are ready but I don't
know if I am ready physically or mentally. I am scared of getting pregnant,
getting an STI, but most of all, rejection!
– Meredith, age 21

While trying to compose an appropriate response to Meredith's letter, I noticed that she originally did not write the word "scared." She had at first written the word "sacred" and then crossed it out. S-A-C-R-E-D. She then drew a line through it. In my reply, I wrote, "Dear Meredith, you had it right the first time!"

The day you can write the words 'I am sacred' on a piece of paper, notice it and not cross it out is the day you can have a conversation about your readiness for sex. This does not mean that you are no longer scared. This does not mean that other people in relationships know they are sacred and you do not. This does not mean that you are actually ready to have sex. This simply means that you notice and acknowledge something unalterable and indestructible living inside you.

Who has the right to see you naked, physically and more importantly, emotionally? Do you look for your partners' sacredness when they take off their clothes? Do you seek out your partners' sacredness when they take off their skin? Sex brings you closer not only to your partner, but to yourself as well. Are you ready to be that naked in front of yourself? When I was in that apartment at the top of the stairs feeling invisible, yet all too visible, I never asked myself these questions. Most of all, I never asked myself if my unsafe sex partner had earned the right to get that close to me.

I dislike my nakedness. I, being a somewhat heavy young woman living in American society, struggle with this issue constantly. I know all too well how it translates into emotional vulnerability. I am always seeking male attention to affirm that I am attractive, even when I know it's from people not remotely worthy and sometimes dangerous. And I have often heard the words, "I Love You," in "You're Beautiful."
– Estefania, age 18

At a university lecture in Texas, a fraternity member sat motionless in his seat long after I had finished speaking. After signaling me to approach, he told me his story. "I am the guy in my frat who tells the other brothers, the initiates and the freshmen pledges, that if they want to get some action they should go for the girls who look like they don't get any. You know," he said, "the ones who are ugly or overweight. They will be so glad you asked." He brought his hands together as if he were measuring his words. "After hearing Meredith's letter, I now see that if I had a little sister at this school and one of my frat brothers so much as thought of her in that way, that would make him an asshole, don't you think?" I nodded my head in agreement. "And that," he continued, "makes me an asshole." His delivery picked up in pace as the thoughts in his head started making sense. "It's not enough that I know I am sacred," he reflected.

"I have to see her as sacred."

Wonderful me, that they can't see
Strong black queen, but I am not lean
A figure to adore, but I ain't a size 4
My build very chic, yet I am not petite

A beautiful girl dismissed and ignored
Tossed out the door
Because my body, which is me
Is more
– Dinean, age 20

There is an expression in Hebrew in which many teenagers believe: 'smokh allai,' which means 'rely on me.' After teaching in an Israeli high school, a 12th grade student came up to talk to me in private. He told me that he was waiting to get his HIV test results at the end of the week.

"My girls," he exclaimed. "What if I have infected my girls." He was wearing an all black outfit and had a splash of glitter on his face. "I'm very popular and many of the 10th and 11th grade girls tell me to come over to their house after school so they can lose their virginity." While talking to me, he did admit to be willing to change a little, now that he was scared that he might have infected some of them. In trying to help him find the best way to value himself and his partners I asked, "What is the Hebrew word for sacred?"

"Kadosh," he replied. "It also means holy, separate and unique."

"Then you must see your 'girls' as holy, separate and unique." I tried to explain that people have sex for many reasons: exploration, intimacy, power, boredom, addiction, lust, energy, money, attention, loneliness, confusion, hormones, reproduction, curiosity, conversation and of course, love. But in order to build a life of sexual integrity, you must become aware of the powerful things moving through you of which you become both participant and witness. It is a taking to deeper waters nearer and nearer to the sacred in you and in your partner. "You could do more than get some action," I instructed. "You could offer your holiness and seek her holiness in return." He nodded his head, promised to use a condom in the future and, before he turned away, offered to email me with his test results. I never heard from him again and I never heard from any of his "girls."

Sex is something that seems to have no value for so many of my friends.
Yet I believe it can be the most desecrating or enlightening experience
you can have. I know that I, like many other males, are expected to be
sexual machines yet I want people to realize it's okay to bust the mold and
wait, like I did, for the right time with someone you love and you know
loves you back.
– Kevin, age 16

A twelve year-old girl in New Jersey posed a conundrum. "I like that letter from Meredith," she began. "And now, when I am old enough to date, I will know that I am sacred and I will see the person I am dating as sacred. But how will I know if the person I'm dating sees me as sacred?" This is something with which many teenagers, introduced to the essence of faith, secretly struggle. I think the bigger question, however, is: how will you know if they see you at all? My friend Dave once said, "The affirmation of a life well-lived is having one or two friends whose faces light up every time you walk into a room." When you call your friends on the phone, listen to the song in their voice as they learn that it's you on the other end. When you send an email, notice how quickly they return it. When your date says "I'll call you," does he? When your girlfriend looks at you, does she see the dynamics of your spirit? Does he see you in a way differently from everyone else? Does she listen better than others? Are you held in their hearts when you are away from them? Do they notice when you're gone?

What does it mean to be sacred? In my
travels, I took a survey and gathered some answers from my many students:

Being noticed by God
Being comfortable with yourself
Not trying to change yourself for anyone regardless of what others say
To be whatever you want to be
Living up to your expectations
Following your dreams

Thinking twice on who I am
Taking in all parts of life, not just the easy, but also the hard
To know that you exist with all that is inside of you,
          the good and the not so good
Being true to yourself
The unchanging parts of yourself
I'm not too fond of the word but I do have lots of respect
          for its meaning
Succinctly put, "I, myself, am more Divine than any I see."

I don't know if I can say "I am sacred" out loud and convince myself yet. Maybe I will soon. I still have trouble with that because I don't really believe I am. I have not always loved myself. I was taught by others that I was second rate. I was the dork, the nerd, the one that no girl was interested in, the one that no boy wanted to call their comrade. I was constantly picked on and tortured. Starting high school, I learned to accept myself and that was a start. Now I must learn to love myself. I want to keep others safe as much as I want to keep myself safe. But I am still not a great person. I don't care for everybody I know. I have angst and some hate. I don't think I qualify as sacred.
– Charlie, age 15

Nicholas is a college student in the northeast who further elaborates:

Sometimes I feel like I am the only one who doesn't feel sacred or doesn't think about the fact that I might be. Sometimes I come away with a feeling of hollowness, as if I am missing something in my life. I don't know what it is but I realize that it's gone. My life just doesn't feel sacred. How does one learn to feel it? I don't know if I can really learn or really understand what it is until I am forced to do so and that scares me. I suppose that being scared is really part of it though. It takes seeing your vulnerability to understand your sacredness.

Sonja is a high school student who writes about her "internal frown:"

I can believe that as a human being and as a living creature I deserve respect and fair treatment. But calling myself sacred...well, that was an idea I lost years ago. I'm just not ready to call myself that.

Finally, Miguel is an adult in his thirties who proves that certain insecurities are not worn out by time:

I don't always remember to hold myself sacred, especially when I'm single and alone and wondering what's wrong with me because no one wants to be with me. I know I am a nice guy, a quality person with a lot going for me and who has a lot to offer. But when I get depressed, because I feel a lack of fulfillment or purpose, whether in my love life, my home life or just my life in general, I start devaluing myself. And that sometimes ends up with my whoring around and too often it's with people that I would want to have nothing to do with normally. But at that moment I need some kind of validation, even valuation, or if I can't get that, then at least immediate gratification. I know these tricks don't love me and I certainly don't love them, but it's company and companionship for right then. And afterwards I feel cheap and slutty and often enough the sex wasn't all that good anyway. But it doesn't stop me from doing it all over again when that mood hits me the next time.

The opposite of sacredness is not disgrace.
It is not failure. It is not confusion. Just because we don't feel sacred does not mean that we are not sacred. Sacredness is not political correctness. Nor is it being perfect, doing it the right way, living the life our parents would approve of or even believing in God. The part of you that is sacred is not the part that is consummate or pure. It is not about chastity or an ostensible sense of holiness. It has nothing to do with having an awesome basketball game, the straightest hair or the highest grade point average in your class. It is not measured by your driving record, your parent's income or your body weight.

I'm sure that everyone tells you why they're not sacred and I could think of a million reasons why I'm not. But I'm going to tell you why I AM sacred. Because most of my pants don't fit me. Because I eat more than most people do or at least more than my friends eat in public. Because I have a hard time trying to figure out what I want to wear. Because I care when people talk about me. I care that I can't do my hair and care what I act like. Because I admit it, I'm insecure, just like everyone else.
– Randi, age 17

The part of you that is sacred is the part that is searching.

It is the part caught in the struggle to reclaim a holiness you think you have lost or given away or were never born with. The sacredness in you is the searching for connection to the sacredness in others who are searching for connection to the sacredness in others. It is an alliance of hope, a union with others who seek a common voice. It is part of the ground you walk upon and the air in your lungs.

To be sacred is to include the fear and the unknown into your experience of life. It is found in moments of woundedness as well as in times of achievement. It is becoming acquainted with the notion that you do not have to be put back together at all. Being broken, being confused, being a contradiction is normal. Sacredness is making room for acceptance of such doubt.

It is not up to you to decide whether or not you are sacred; it is up to you to accept, encompass and embrace that you are sacred. A mother from Massachusetts writes, "Casey held up her cell phone this morning and announced that she had deleted all the phone numbers of the guys who do not see her as sacred!"

Sacredness is the source of your true reality. It is the movement of spirit within a heart that is unanchored by loss. Yet it is also the unfolding of delight within and the lift you give to victory.

When it seems that life has been reckless with your dreams and you feel abandoned by God, you are still sacred. When you are confused and when you are victorious, you are still sacred. When you are in a state of negative self-judgment or positive self-approval, you are sacred. In your loneliness or sense of desolation, you are sacred. In your glory and resplendency, you are sacred.

I salute you all that you stand for, struggle with and believe.

You are always sacred.

Jordan

At lunch time Jordan threw his bookbag over his shoulder, walked out the heavy metal double-doors at the end of the corridor and went over to his favorite spot. It was a tiny duck pond surrounded by a circular driveway leading up to the entrance to his school. Hunched down with his knees nearly touching the ground, he sat back on his ankles and threw pieces of a leftover peanut butter and jelly sandwich into the water. I hunched down next to him in silence.

"You found me," Jordan said, turning his face away to hide his crescent smile. We passed pieces of his half-eaten sandwich between us and watched the fish poke at the surface of the water. We talked about God, his girlfriend and his future. "Tell me this," he said, staring straight out in front of him. "Is it okay not to worry about 9th grade math since Algebra is useless once you graduate high school, anyway?"

I smiled. "Nice try," I said as we watched the uneaten bread shrivel and float on the surface of the pond, surrounded by bottle caps and branches.

"If you could have one wish," he asked, "would it have anything to do with AIDS?" But before I could speak he said, "There's nothing I really need," answering his own question. "I mean, if I had only the one wish in life...then I kind of realize that I don't really need any wishes at all." I brushed off the dirt and debris from the back of his shirt as we started walking back to class. We talked some more about his girlfriend, about religion and about his impending break-up with her because of her parent's religious beliefs. We talked about the lines people draw between others in their lives when it comes to dating and why they draw them in the first place. We talked and talked about football and big sisters, hip/hop music and the latest fashion trends and all the other major issues underlying the true meaning of life. When I asked about the key hanging from a chain around his neck, he answered, "It's the key to open everyone's heart."

I visit Jordan's school every six months so I was familiar with his inquisitive mind. Jordan had a knack, he did, of laying out all the questions in his universe and gradually honing in on the one issue that concerned him directly. "I've got a problem," he finally submitted, as we neared the front steps to the school. "My girlfriend doesn't believe in having sex until she's married." He paused for a second, trying to add gravity to his next sentence. "I can't wait that long. All my friends are having sex. Troy is having sex; Carlos is having sex. I think I should be doing it too. I mean, I am fourteen years-old after all."

He looked past me, back out onto the pond and continued speaking. "My ex-girlfriend told me that she wants to have sex with me this weekend. She told me online in an Instant Message. So I know it's true. I don't know what to do. Should I have sex with her? I don't love her anymore. I mean, she's my ex-girlfriend and all...and you don't love your ex's, right? But my two closest friends say it's the greatest thing in the world. Am I missing out?"

Later that day after school ended, we sat in an ice cream parlor to finish our conversation. The place was empty, except for our waitress and an eighty-five year-old man in a red and white striped shirt playing Disney songs on an organ. Over two super-sized sundaes and a pitcher of water we dissected Jordan's dilemma. "If you want to know if you should have sex with your ex, I can't tell you. That's not my job," I said. "That's up to you to decide for yourself. But maybe I can give you some guidance. Let's see if you can come up with answers to some questions I have for you. This might help you see if you are ready."

Jordan carved a huge hole into one side of his sundae and lifted the spoon, already dripping over with melted ice cream. "First," I began, "have you kissed her?"

"Have I kissed her?" he smiled, wiping the warm butterscotch off his face. "Of course I've kissed her! She's my ex-girlfriend."

"Okay, then," I continued, "have you seen her naked?" Again Jordan smiled. "Yeah, I've seen her naked. This is easy. Okay, what's number three?"

"Number three," I responded, "Has she seen you naked?" Without a beat he dropped his spoon into his dish and, donning an air of self-imposed nobility, proudly announced, "Everybody's seen me naked!" I laughed out loud and reached for a spoonful of coffee ice-cream. Feeling refreshed by the sweetness of chocolate covered sprinkles mixed with long afternoon conversations and teenagers in the throes of infatuation, I thought about how to pose my next question. "So, answer me this. Have you gone down on her?"

"What's that?" he asked innocently.

"Jordan," I continued, leaning in, almost whispering, "there's an eighty-five year old man in the corner playing *It's a Small World After All.* I don't know how else to put this. Have you... you know... performed oral sex?" He sat back and thought about it for a moment and then shouted, "Uhhhch! That's disgusting, man. I just want to get some ass!"

And the music stopped.

Here before me was a boy who had not yet realized that sex

has many other elements besides desire and impulse.
He had not yet reached an understanding that sex is more
than the actual act of penetration, but also something people
do to one another's bodies that involves both the spiritual as
well as the physical. He had not yet experienced the sanctity
of consequence: that sexual activity engages the history of
another person's heart and makes an everlasting imprint
upon another person's soul. Emotion of such nature, from such
an act, once experienced and assimilated into the psyche, can
sometimes leave behind a malevolent residue: the inexorable
afterburn of young love.

I went to pay for the ice cream. Sitting on top of the counter
alongside the register was an assortment of colorful jars filled
with candies: long strands of red licorice, dark chocolate
non-pareils and gourmet flavored jellybeans. Jordan approached
me with two lollipops in his left hand and some loose change in
the other. "I need twenty-five more cents," he said appealingly.
"If I had a quarter, that would be so great, 'cause then I'd have
enough money to buy three lollipops. And I would really love
to have three lollipops."

I looked into his face as I reached into the front left pocket of
my jeans, put a quarter into his open hand and smiled. "Three
is so much better than two," he added.

Here before me was a child on the cusp, a kid in the candy store of life getting ready to savor all the treats, yet not quite ready to sustain all the trials, that growing up engenders.

While driving him home I realized that adolescence is often-times the ungraceful art of leave-taking, the long mournful wave goodbye to the naive world of childhood's sweet unawarenesses. It is an emptying of hands and an opening of arms, a relinquishing and a reaching. Daring the heart to beat faster, we leave a part of ourselves behind in surrendering an early identity. Daring the heart to break, we welcome the unexplored self, just about to arrive. Standing on the midway, we are told that these are the best years of our lives and, as adolescents, we have the audacity to believe it, trying to enjoy life in spite of its demanding circumstances.

Jordan sat next to me in the front seat of my rental car and offered up a few more fragments from the universe of his questioning mind.

"Do you believe in God?"
"Do you ever regret getting infected with HIV?"
"Are you dying?"

"Jordan," I said, "I visit with you twice a year and every time we get together you ask the same three questions." He fidgeted with the knobs on the radio, changing and resetting all my pre-programmed stations. "I know," he answered, "but I'm getting older and I need to hear the old answers with my new mind."

As I maneuvered my hand and forearm against the steering wheel, leaning into the curves in the road ahead, I remembered conversations on car rides in my long ago past; conversations between my dad and big brother. Robert always got to ride shotgun, "because I'm older," he would boldly pronounce. And I, sitting in the backseat of boyhood, witnessing a private dialogue between a father and his son, would listen longingly.

"Da," he once said, posing a question. "If God exists, then why did He make us have fear?" My father always had an answer for Robert and this time was no different. He responded instanta-neously, "So that we don't hurt one another." I loved that answer and I loved my father for his ever and always all-knowingness. Softly, almost at the level of a whisper, I added, "Especially so that we don't hurt ourselves." And then, in the recesses of my mind I commanded myself, "I'm going to be like him one day."

Now sitting in my once-imagined future, I answered each of Jordan's questions. "Yes, I believe in God. I believe that God is sitting right in between us with one hand on each of our shoulders, listening to each of us as we speak. And I don't blame myself for getting infected with HIV, not anymore, because I never would have otherwise met you, or any of the other teenagers I have been blessed to meet."

Studying the road before us, I attended to his third and most important question. "Am I dying? Jordan," I said as I glanced over to him, "I am as alive now as I ever need to be. This is life. This car ride. This moment and this memory. This connection. And with you and this road before us, it's enough."

As we pulled into the driveway of his parent's house, he asked to see the letter that Meredith wrote about being sacred. "I think that if I could actually see the word she crossed out... the word 'sacred'... I think that will help me." So I reached into the backseat for my scrapbook of letters and emails and opened it to the page he requested. There on the facing page, before her letter, was an email Jordan had written on the day he met his ex-girlfriend. "Dear Scott," he wrote, "I met a girl and I don't know how to ask her out. Can you help me find the words to get her to say 'yes' to me?" Ironically, on the very next page of my scrapbook was his help in finding the way to say 'no' to sex with her.

"Do you think Meredith knew what she was doing when she wrote this letter?" he asked while tracing the scripted word upon the written page with his fingers. "I mean, do you think she knew that she was sacred and then maybe changed her mind when she saw it on the paper and crossed it? Or do you think it was a mistake?"

"I don't know, Jordan." I answered. "But I guess it doesn't really matter what she thought. What matters right now is what you think. Jordan, are you sacred?" He looked up at the roof of my rental car and as if he, in the Emerald City of his mind, were clicking his heels three times, recited aloud, "I am sacred. I am sacred, I am sacred." Then, as if a thunderbolt of resoluteness had suddenly struck from deep within, he announced, "You know what? I'm not having sex with my ex this weekend!"

Trying to hide my immeasurable sense of relief, I posed a question. "Why not?"

"Well," he answered, straightening himself in his seat, like a teenager after a growth spurt trying on a starched suit in a larger size, "I thought about your questions and saw Meredith's letter and well, ..."

"Yes, Jordan?"

"...well, the way I see it...you know what? She doesn't deserve me!"

It was a school night and he needed to get started on his homework, but I could tell he was searching for ways to delay his leaving. "I just need to find the perfect song," he said as he scanned the stations on the radio. "Oh I love this song," he exclaimed. "Dave Matthews! *Crash Into Me*. Cool." He held onto the door handle with his right hand, listened to a few verses of the song and tapped his foot. "Thanks for the ice cream. And the talk," he said liltingly. "I'll email you; I promise." Then, within the next instant, he was gone.

I put the car into reverse and began backing out of his parent's driveway. As I raised the volume on the radio and then looked over my shoulder into the street behind me, I listened attentively to the lyrics of Jordan's new favorite song: "Hike up your skirt a little more and show your world to me - in a boy's dream."

Suddenly, I heard a tap on my windshield; it was Jordan once more. Stopping the car, I rolled down the window and readied myself for his final parting words. "One more thing. Tell all your students what I learned in school today. I want everyone to know what I learned, which is written somewhere in the Talmud:

"Days are like scrolls. Write thereon only what you would like to have remembered about you."

Dear Scott,

My name is Lauren and I'm a teenager. I have this amazing capability of metamorphosing my disposition at a moment's notice. I have many insecurities that I am incapable of expressing. I look in the mirror and I am repulsed by the reflection. I doubt myself; I question others. Welcome to my secret world.

Before my dreams whisk me away to faraway lands, I lie in bed and mull over the emotions that whirl around in my brain. I question my thoughts, my ethics and my beliefs. I question the meaning of life. Despite the hundreds of kids that flood the hallways of my school, I have yet to discover a single soul that has the same ideals, insecurities and feelings as me. Though, I must say, I've come remarkably close. Am I alone in this agonizing and tortuous growth into adulthood? They say these are the best years of your life. Who are "they" anyway? I envy them.

I don't want you to misinterpret my adolescent confusion for immaturity. High school has been an unforgettable experience. I had my first boyfriend, my first kiss and my first best friend. There is one thing lacking, though, as my days of childhood come to a close. I haven't yet established who I am.

If you were to look up the word "timid" in the dictionary you would find a picture of me in the middle of the definition. I've never skipped school. I've never been drunk and

I've never done drugs. I've always been shy and modest. Authority kind of dismays me. One of my biggest concerns is disappointing people. I hate getting into fights or disagreements with others. It seems as though I'm more concerned with their opinions than my own. It's a fear I someday hope to vanquish. I've always felt out of place. Even when I was five years-old there were always the other kids who seemed to know more than me. It was as if they knew a secret that someone forgot to tell me. I was just "the watcher." I observed everything and I still do. I hide behind a face that never stops smiling. I fear the day that I am exposed because behind this mask I wear lies a tangled web of insecurities.

So here I am, a senior in high school who sometimes feels the same way she did in kindergarten. While most of my friends are itching to go off on their own, I'm not ready to go to college. I'm still afraid to walk alone in the dark let alone live in a dorm over three hundred miles away. Yet I am only one person in a sea of faces. You could pass me on the street and not think twice about it. However, my day-to-day experiences define me, and they make my world go 'round. And while my world is spinning out of control, you probably wouldn't even feel the ground move. Someday I hope to look in the mirror and smile. I hope to speak my mind without hesitation. I hope to love being me. In time. For now you can just label me "a work in progress."

— Lauren, age 17

Dear Scott,

I have this friend and her entire life she's had problems,
be they sex, drugs or cutting. I have helped her through
all these crises and have seen their impact on her life and
I can't help but say, "I wish I was her." I wish
I had these problems so all these people, all these boys,
would want to fix me. I used to see the world in a
two-valued semantic light: you are working or you are
broken, and if you're broken someone will fix you.
People with problems always seem to lead extraordinary
lives with the happy ending.

— Heather, age 17

11 | *the abc's of* self-care

If you could be the healthiest you have ever been in body, mind and spirit, what would you be like? What would you do differently? How would you get through a crisis?

Self-neglect can breed unfair expectations of the world. We anticipate that others will do for us what is really ours to do for ourselves. When you don't take care of yourself, you may find that you want someone else to inappropriately do it for you. When you don't take special notice of your inner life, you may find that you will disproportionately want people to notice it. When you don't attend to your own needs, you may start unfairly expecting others to attend to them. And when "the others" don't come through, you get to hold a grudge and say,

"See? I was right. I AM invisible."

Asking for help is paramount to a life of sound self-care. But to a certain degree, validation of self is not anyone else's job but our own. When we take responsibility for some of our pain, it begins to go away. However, instead of always conducting ourselves in a healthy manner, sometimes we get foolhardy with our lives and our bodies. For some, our "drug of choice" is a single act of defiance; for others, it can be a co-occurrence of risky behaviors. Whatever the method, a lack of routine self-care can lead to contamination of the invisible kingdom.

I always expected everyone to fix everything because I didn't know how to do it myself. Everyone else seems to make the impossible look possible. I was so desperate to find someone who had figured it out that I never realized there was no genie coming to grant me my three wishes. There was and is only me, but I didn't know where or who "me" was and I never thought it would be okay for me to be clueless. All I did know was I had to find myself to heal myself. Not to find a way out but to find a way to actually feel I'm still okay. I realized that, in order to allow myself to begin living again, I have to set myself free from the deception, the lies and all the denial haunting my every move. I'm beginning to awaken from the darkness that has so long surrounded me, not always wishing for change but finding happiness somewhere in the destiny I've been handed. Today I am without

answers but less confused than before. In no way can I say I'm where I want or need to be but finally I have an idea of the direction I need to go.
– Kelly, age 20

Here is my list of instructions for a healthier life of self-care:

Action. Feel your feelings, then do something. Brush your teeth. Do your homework. Feed your goldfish. Answer your email. Pay your bills. Tie your shoes. Drink your milk. Eat your dinner. Call your mother. Attend to whatever is in front of you and stay responsible. Regardless of your pain, do something. Eventually, the seemingly tedious tasks will become gifts to get you through the day. Jonathan from Florida says, "The way I see it, there's nothing bigger than the little things. Life is in the details."

I will only live until tomorrow
Until tomorrow becomes today
I will only live until tomorrow
– Sam, age 15

Believe. Faith is itself the act of asking for faith. Cast your net far and wide and allow the universe to work for you. Believe that there is magic in you. Believe in something. Your dreams. The stars. Your screen name. One teenager's screen name read 'Butgodisnowhere.' Upon first inspection, it reads "but God is nowhere." But if you look closely, it can also read, "But God is Now Here."

Every minute that you don't spend appreciating the good things you have is a minute you could be closer to losing those very things without the recognition they deserve. We must take advantage of every opportunity we have to express our love, to spend time together, to search for that piece of faith that is within all of us. It is up to all of us to live each moment together and never forget who and what means most. Things can be replaced; people cannot.
– Michael, age 20

Compassion. Always be kind and gentle. As you grow, there will be much that people will want to share with you and show you, but they will be afraid because vulnerability is a scary thing. Help them carry the burden of life's lessons and assist them to find room for joy alongside of pain. Your compassion and goodness will tell them that it's okay to be fragile. In that way, they can be made to feel safe again. Sam is a fifteen year-old from Washington DC with "out of the bottle" dyed green hair. "They say, 'It's not easy being green,'" he told me, "but I needed to find out for myself." One of the ways to break the cycle of inward aggression is to treat ourselves with the same compassion we would offer someone else that we love. Where is the compassion for yourself? Sometimes, there are no right or wrong answers or actions, only opportunities to do things differently. Ask yourself, is this working or is there a better way?

You know you are grown up when your heart feels deeper and you
start to care more about people. More than I want to help the people that
are hurting, I want to help the people that are making them hurt!
—Yvonne, age 17

Dream. When life gives you a multiple choice question, answer (D) all of above.

There is so much more out there. I can feel it. I can taste it.
It haunts my dreams. I want it all.
—Haley, age 19

Exercise. Get into an on-going, consistent routine that you employ every day of your life. Exercise helps channel your energy in positive and healthy ways, relieves stress and anxiety and gives you a chance to take care of your body at the same time. We all internalize our issues in different ways and learn to handle our emotions through many different methods. The most important thing is to figure out what works best for you. Some people like to deal with problems and stresses by playing sports, walking their dog or going for a run. Whatever you do, as long as it helps to relieve your anxiety and focuses your attention on the betterment of your mind, body and spirit, will be true self-help and care.

I use exercise and physical fitness as my method of self-help. I go to the gym
everyday; I have a trainer; I take exercise classes; I do yoga and I like to
go on walks, hike, swim and dance. For me, expending extra energy and
built-up tension through movement and action works the best. When I go to
the gym, I leave my cell phone in the car, take my headphones and favorite

CD's and only allow myself to bring fun reading material. In this way, I always associate fun and freedom with exercise and fitness. Exercise helps me prepare for my day by allowing me time in the morning to sort my thoughts and figure out my plans. It helps me sit still in class by giving me a means to expel the extra energy I would normally not know what to do with during the day. It gets my blood flowing and sends those much needed endorphins rushing through my body. It clears my head and relieves pent-up stress and anxiety. And of course, it keeps me in shape and helps me stay healthy. I have come to depend on this hour and a half everyday. No one can bother me and nothing can upset me. Even if you can't get to a gym or don't have a free hour-and-a-half everyday, take some time to go on a walk, to take a run or to do some stretching and breathing exercises. Over time and with consistency, you will feel better – mentally, emotionally and of course, physically.
– Amy, age 20

Fear.
Be willing to be afraid. Chris is a teen in a Juvenile Detention Center who writes, "I am scared, but I don't say that to people because I don't want to sound like a little kid." Fear is just adrenaline, another color with which to paint onto the canvas of your world. Learn to live with it. Fear is the thing that helps you finish crossing the street. It is not who you are; it is just what's visiting you, sometimes emboldening you. Honor it because it makes you accessible. As eighteen year-old Marc says, "I live my life in fear. That's why I live my life." What's the point of fear if it doesn't help you grow stronger?

The undeniable truth remains that I am scared that I won't fit in. I am scared that my parents will ground me next weekend. I am scared that I wont receive honor roll on my next report card. But it's okay to be scared and it's okay to make mistakes. I don't need to test my problem-free blessings. I feel that by trusting these facts I can truly value my life as well as the lives of others.
– Krista, age 16

Gratitude.
Alfonso is a teenager who said, "I have been thinking about all the things that I have been blessed with in this life. Gratitude brings with it a strange peace that I forget was always there. I now see how

much we would win if we only learned to be grateful for all the things we have in life."

I was walking home from the gym one morning feeling very dizzy and uncomfortable, trudging through the gross, slushy streets where mud was gathering on my shoes. I was about to say, "Uch, this is such an awful day," when all of a sudden I realized that I am able to feel the slushy rain on my feet and able to walk to and from the gym. I am here right now. It was as if the ground began to sparkle making it seem like jewels were coming up from the mud. I was able to take a bad day and turn it into a beautiful experience.
– Gretchen, age 16

Heart. Love, as a verb. As an action. As a daily task. Especially love those who are hardest to love, for they need it the most. Sometimes love hurts. It gives you ground only to take it out from under you, making you chase after it. Keep chasing it. Joe is a cab driver in Illinois who once said, "I'm nothing special. You can cross me out, you can beat me up but you cannot kill my love. I'm someone who is able to tell people that I love them." Sandy is a wise friend who keeps reminding me to "love the averageness in all people." And finally, Doug is a teenager with unbounded instinct who says, "Love makes you not an asshole."

I'm still waiting for that answer to how learning "integration rules" in my calculus class will leave me infinitely more prepared to make some profound contribution to the betterment of society and my own personal life. Since when does calculus matter at 3:30 in the morning when you're lying awake, wrapped tight in the arms of a person whom you love so much that you can hardly bear it, listening to the sound of the inhalations and exhalations as they sleep peacefully beside you? Last time I checked, THOSE were the moments and people and events that actually matter in this world. The moments and loves and realizations that teach us and remind us why we're here.
– Michelle, age 20

Individuality. Try being single for a while.

I used to hang onto 'the last guy' until the next guy came around. It may not be the most comforting thought but I have learned that it is okay to not have someone to call to say 'goodnight' every evening or someone around

when I wake up in the morning. It is okay to be alone. It is okay to be single. It is more than okay to give 100% of myself to myself. Now I can let go of the 'last guy' simply by being happy in and of myself. It's scary and it's a challenge, but it should be really good for me.
– Andrea, age 18

Joy. Make a list of the things that bring you special joy.

The red stains on my fingers after eating too many pistachio nuts
"My So Called Life" marathons
When people compliment me on looking good
The smell of rain
Having no classes during "General Hospital"
Numbers 6 through 10
The sound of ice cubes in a glass of iced tea
A good game of Scrabble
A wool blanket placed over me in the middle of a nap
Milk Duds in the movies
Outdoor showers
The extra second stare someone takes when you know they like you
Realizing your life is pretty good after all
–Traci, age 21

Kindness. As you proceed on into the future, let kindness be the legacy you leave behind. At my twentieth high school reunion, an old friend approached me with thanks for being so kind to her in sixth grade. "Those were the days when Ritalin was scarce," she laughed. "You were the one person who never made fun of my tantrums. I've always remembered you for that."

There is this one kid in my grade who my group of friends torment because he different. I was always really nice to him, but he always gave me the cold shoulder and I never knew why. Then I remembered all the times I stood by and watched while he got hurt and never did anything to stop it. I didn't do anything but notice. I never said a word. I realize that sometimes standing by not doing anything at all can be worse than doing the crime itself. I was so ashamed to be part of a group of people that made someone feel that way. Were there more kids that felt the same? What really bothered me is that he probably could be one of the most interesting people I would ever get to

know in high school but I blew whatever chance I had to become his friend. So I wrote him a letter and slipped it to him at the end of class. In it I wrote everything because I figured honesty might be the best solution. He wrote back with two simple words, "Thank you." I can't tell you how good that felt. I learned that it doesn't matter who your friends are and what the consequences will be if you do something differently from them. If you know something is right, stand up for your beliefs and don't worry what people say about you. As long as you know that you did the right thing, you won't have any regrets.
– Maggie, age 16

Loneliness. Lonely people are not always found in lonely places. You may breathe the same air, walk on the same side of the street and eat the same cafeteria food as everyone else, yet they may also harbor their very own secrets, sorrows and insecurities.

Having ADD (Attention Deficit Disorder) can sometimes make me feel like an outsider; everything is a hundred times harder for me. I study three hours for a quiz so I can pass when my friends study for only one hour and get 90s. I feel inferior and inadequate to everyone else. I wonder, does the guy sitting across from me in math who is real smart when he talks but is always looking out the window, does he have the same feelings? Does the girl in my gym class with no coordination in volleyball and is always alone all the time, does she feel the same way? Do my friends? Are they as lonely as me?
– Judy, age 15

As you lament the unspent hours with unmet companions, know that you are enough. Bless you for your unspoken pain. For your hidden auto-biography. For trying to make sense of this thing they call "growing up." In the game of love and loneliness, you only win if you realize the two go hand in hand. One earns the other and in the end you are a better person for it, the kind of person that a special someone deserves.

Mistakes. Value your mistakes; there is merit in stumbling. Appraise the alternatives. Sara is a teen figure skater released from the hospital after treatment for anorexia who said, "I figure if I have to be 95 pounds to do a triple axle turn, then I'll learn to play ice hockey."

No one ever told me that it was okay to fail before. In fact, failure was the one thing that I was scared of more than anything, (with the possible exception of spiders). But somewhere, amidst the feelings of loneliness, confusion and failure, there is a glimmer of hope that things will get better.
– Yanina, age 18

The four "Nevers" in relationships:

Never trust anyone who says, "You can trust me." Trust must be earned, not taken.

Never say to anyone, "I'll never leave you." That's a promise you may not be able to keep.

Never use modern technology to do your dirty work. Don't break-up with someone over the phone, in an email or text message. Have the decency to do it in person.

Never tell someone, "I don't love you anymore." If you are able to say that, then you never did at all.

Get to know me. Allow me to be unique. Give me the chance to show you who I am. Respect my boundaries. When I say "No," it's not a game to get me to say "Yes." I'm not a trophy or a toy.
– Anonymous

Obey. Simply put, when you are driving, slow down.

Last night I got a speeding ticket on the way home doing 77 mph in a 55 mph zone and almost put the car in a ditch pulling off the road. It's not the ticket that bothers me most, but the fact that I didn't realize I was going so fast and hadn't paid attention to the limits and my surroundings. I learned many important things last night: not to think about distracting topics while driving; when the highway is two-lane the speed limit is slower than four-lane; and cops can come out of nowhere. The ticket is $175.10 and I lost 6 points on my license. But more than that, I lost credibility in the eyes of the people I love. I learned the hard and expensive way, but I learned. Now I have to deal with it: my fault, my consequences.
– Shannon, age 17

Prioritize.

In this instant, everything is fine. Right now is all that matters. Right here is everything you need - this moment, this opening, this enough-ness. Whenever you feel fear and worry, take a look inside and realize that your mind is probably running away with the present tense and chasing scenes that do not yet exist. All you have is this moment. What can you learn from it? How much can you squeeze out of it before it turns into the future? Celebrate this instant. Swim in the immediacy of the present. Be in the now for now.

*"When I'm with you, I am constantly building a wall preparing for
the moment when you decide I am not the one for you," he announced
plainly, much as if he had asked me to pass the butter at dinner.
As he turned to leave I whispered, "I do love you. The problem is that
I feel you are living for an uncertain time in the future and I am living
in today." In building one great world for our future, he was building
many little walls in the present.*
– Morgan, age 23

Qualify.

Try not to compare yourself to others; praise them instead. If you can witness it, you can be it. See your competitors as teachers and guides, the mirror to your potential. Allow others their success and you will be allowing yourself your own.

Success is reaching the top of a mountain with someone on your shoulders.
– Brandon, age 16

Responsibility.

Learn how to put your needs above everyone else's once in awhile. Concentrate on the things that pertain to your daily survival. Sometimes saying 'no' will help you to regain balance and keep you safe regardless of what others may say or think. Ask yourself, "What's my part in this?"

*Last night I was in the back of an Explorer with six guys, (one was my
boyfriend and the other five I didn't know since they don't go to my school).
We were going to the basketball game when they decided they needed some
pot. It was extremely foggy and we couldn't see five feet in front of us.
Everyone, including me, was high and the guys decided to race. We were
going 100 mph down country roads and no one was wearing a seat belt.*

*I started getting really scared. Then I asked myself a lot of questions like,
"Do I deserve to be in a situation like this? Do I hate myself so much to
risk my life doing stupid things? Am I worth more than this?" I knew
then that if I stayed on that track I would eventually end up killing myself.
I got dropped off immediately, ran to my room and laid on the bed crying.
I don't know how my life is going to go from here, but I do know that
I'm not going to be in a situation like that ever again.*
– Marquita, age 17

Support.
In the early days of my HIV infection, I became a
support group junkie going to an AIDS meeting or support session every
day of the week - individual therapy, group therapy, couple's counseling,
inspirational lectures, weekend workshops and/or retreats. Groups of people
sitting around a room and sharing their daily struggles by talking and
listening to each other can really help. Talk about your fears. Talk about
your fantasies and foibles. Talk about anything and everything. The world
needs to hear your truth so keep talking. My friend Billy says, "You don't
get extra points for going through this life alone."

*In the last few years, my little sister was diagnosed with ocular melanoma,
a rare cancer that starts in the eye, which then spread to her liver and
then into a tumor on her lung. It wasn't her being in the hospital that
was the worst part. It was having nowhere to go without people in school
bringing it up. It was like her cancer had become my whole identity.
The sympathetic glances in school were more than I could take. Was
the word "weak" or "victim" written all over my face? Tired of feeling
helpless and being seen as helpless, I got ready to ask for support. I started
with my Social Actions club at school. I got up in front of the whole club
and just started talking. I told them everything. I think I fell into some
kind of a trance because I was not too aware of what I'd said. I just
remember looking up when I finished and seeing the entire room in tears
and then hearing them say, "How can we help?"*
– Joanne, age 17

Tears.
Give voice to your emotions. As my friend Susan says, "I'm
crying out loud, for crying out loud." Tears have a bad rap in our society.
Notice how sometimes a parent will comfort a crying baby with the
words, "Sshh...don't cry." Yet, it is a part of our humanness. The problem

is not that we cry, it's that we don't cry enough. Bless you for your tears.

Oftentimes people tell themselves that it's not okay to be unhappy.
But sadness plays a major role in a person's 'life advances,' growing up in
this globe of craziness; essentially, this sadness makes us who we are today.
"I feel, therefore, I know I am alive," a quote I kind of live by. Boys do cry,
and so do girls. Also men and women and animals, too. Maybe even
God sometimes. Just know this: it's okay to be sad. It's okay to feel.
And it is definitely okay to cry. Keep pushing through the tunnel of
broken hearts, for once you get through angels will heal.
'venni vetti vecci' – I came, I saw, I conquered.
– Jordan, age 15

Understanding. Forgive someone. In fact, forgive everyone;
it will add years to your life. Whether or not you think they deserve it, you
do. When you hold grudges against people, you lock them inside a prison
in your heart. Consequently, there needs to be an emotional warden to
watch over them so they don't escape. It is too much work and takes too
much good energy from you. Set them free and set yourself free.

I've had conversations with myself for years about asking my family
why they separated us from our uncle. I don't know what hurts more,
their keeping his HIV/AIDS status a secret from me or the fact that
I didn't get to go to his funeral. I'm not sure if I can forgive them now
but maybe someday in the future I can. And I'm not exactly sure what
forgiveness is going to feel like. I know I'm not going to get a card in the
mail that says, "Congratulations, you have just forgiven your family!"
I wonder how I'm going to know to recognize it. I hope that I will
somehow feel it inside my heart, a power from within that is
immeasurable, boundless and without limits.
– Aliza, age 17

Remember as well, forgiveness takes time. My friend John Fletcher Harris
used to say, "Forgiveness comes, when it comes, if it comes. Just as you
can't force Mother Nature, forgiveness comes in its own time." For now,
at least be willing to forgive. And while you are working on forgiveness of
others, forgive yourself, for it is just another word for mercy. Go gently
upon your journey through life. In the words of Jared, a college student in
Pennsylvania, "This love of life is what alone ensures my victory."

One evening I was walking down the street and saw myself reflected in a store window and something looked...different. I mean, I looked the same as I always did, but it was like somehow I could tell that I had become someone I had never wanted to be. I spent the next few days just peeling back layer after layer and trying to see if I could find myself. And I did, but forgiving myself for the way I had behaved (by disrespecting myself and those around me) was one of the hardest things I've ever done. I've started to feel a little better about myself. I am reconnecting with who I want to be and I can start to work on living that life again.
– Abe, age 18

Volunteer.
On an envelope from a student named Samantha were written the words, "Everyone you meet is fighting a harder battle." Find something to do for someone else and give your all to it. When you volunteer your time and energy you will meet people who have it harder than you. It will take you out of your head and teach you about the incredible strength of others, and if you can see strength in others, it must be somewhere inside of you as well. Meet someone who has it harder than you and see how he or she survives. They might just say, "You should meet some of my friends who've got it harder than me and see how they survive." And so on and so on.

On a beautiful Sunday morning a little over a week ago, my friends and I stood outside a supermarket collecting items for AIDS patients. I asked everyone going in to pick up an extra item on our list and to donate it on their way out. Last year, we got about two shopping carts filled with items. Last week, in the four hours that we were there, we collected over five shopping carts of items to be donated! We then brought them back to our dorm room and sorted them. Later in the week we drove to the health center in the next city and gave them everything. They were so thrilled with all that we had collected. We essentially restocked their shelves for them. All day, while I handed out flyers and spoke to people, I was thinking of others who need our help. I just wanted to let you know that there are a lot of great people out here that are on their side, helping to fight their battles.
– Elisa, age 19

Withdraw. Don't take it all too personally. Remember that compliments and insults are two sides of the same coin. If you measure your worth by people's praise, you will have to invariably measure it against their criticism of you as well. Stay in your center; it's never really about you, anyway.

If a guy can't handle my twenty extra pounds, then how's he gonna put up with my mood swings?
— Anne, age 17

XYZ. Living a life of self-care can help us to see our part in the larger picture, that we are infinitely linked to others seeking a similar tenderness. It is in our connectedness to one another, in our knowing that our lives are of consequence to others, that we can be healed. When we hurt ourselves, we hurt others who love us. When we take care of ourselves, we are also taking care of those around us.

In allowing ourselves to become strong and comfortable with all that is new and unfamiliar, we can be made to feel safe again.

You belong to this place, this life. You have a right to hurt and a right to heal. Find your own special ground for growing. Seek out ways of loving yourself through the difficult times. And have faith in the future

because you are a part of it.

A Boy, His Dad and a bike

When I was a little boy my father took me by the hand and led me outside to the curb in front of the house. There, on the street outside our door was my red Huffy bicycle with the white vinyl banana seat and the silver bell screwed onto the handlebars. But when I looked at the tires, I saw that my father had removed my training wheels.

He lifted me up onto the seat, steadied me as my sneakers found the grooves in the shiny metal of the pedals and began to push the bike. I remember falling off balance only a few times. With his left hand firmly gripping the handlebars and his right hand glued to the back of my seat, my father ran alongside me and pushed me up the street.

I remember that boy. That boy alone with his dad. I remember feeling emboldened by the smooth newly tarred blacktop under my wheels and the dip in the center of the road. By the smile in his voice. By the scent of his closeness. His cheer.

When I reached the top of the street, he was gone. Mid-journey, mid-glee, without any warning, he let go of the handlebars and went back to the front of the house. He watched me finish the ride alone.

"When did you let go?" I shouted out to him, climbing off the bike and breathlessly searching for the kickstand. "I thought you were with me the whole time."

He waved at me and smiled. "You did it yourself," he yelled back. "You can do it on your own now. I trust you."

Many years later, outside my father's hospital room, I stood next to my mother as she cried.

"I don't have my friend anymore. I miss him already."

Inside his room, I leaned in alongside his bed and listened for his thoughts. "It doesn't look good, does it?"

I squeezed his hand and said, "No Dad, it doesn't. It doesn't look good."

In an instant I was that boy again. That boy alone with his dad. In telling him the truth, I hoped that I had given him permission to look forward. A chance to look with incredible love and gratitude upon his life. To appreciate. To value.

To feel for a moment fully alive

And present
And human
To make it to the top of the street, emboldened by the dip in
the center of the road, the smile in my voice, the scent of
my closeness.

He squeezed my hand. "Scotty. Oh Scotty," was all he said.

My Mom walked into the room and wept into her sleeve.
The patient in the next bed made distracting noises.
My brothers and sister gathered around my dad. We hovered
as he looked off into the distance. We talked about the life
insurance policies, the files in the left-hand side drawer, the
house. He stared off a little while longer. He told us he loved us.

And then he fell asleep.

A week after my father died my mother emptied all the food
from the refrigerator, sat at the kitchen table and wept.
"Mama...mama...why didn't you answer my prayers?" she cried,
looking towards heaven. "Mama...mama...what am I going
to do now?"

In keeping with our tradition, as a way of ending Shivah,
the week-long period of mourning after the funeral, my family
assembled for a ceremonial walk around the block.
The leaves, already surrendering to sorrow, gathered at
our feet. The sun, abdicating its place in the sky, settled on
our backs. With my father's memory pressing against me,
the season of change had begun.

When we reached the top of the street, I looked back for a
second and remembered his words. I imagined him standing by,
smiling at me, waving me on.

And then I turned the corner.

Dear Scott,

Have I told you today how much I love you?
If I have not, let me say it again

I love you forever

Dad

Dear Scott,

My name is Ali and I am afraid of being forgotten.

The heightened awareness of not only myself but the world around me sometimes dissipates in my little insular realm. I don't want it to. And that speaks volumes. So now I write a piece of myself for you, a crease in the palm of existence.

I am not writing this to earn eternal fame in your repository binders of emails.

I am not writing this to ask for an opinion.
I am not writing this for a response.
I am writing to expose the community in
      my own Invisible Kingdom.

My kingdom has vitriolic goblins, fire-breathing dragons, distorting fun house mirrors and moats of electric water.
      But I will not lead you over the drawbridge in.

I am writing to cross the bridge myself.
I am writing because I want to be "seen."

I don't need a bloodshot epiphany of knowledge
I have never realized before. I need a new lens with which
to look at my life. I am not perfect, but no one's mind
or soul is. Isn't life wonderful?

I do not know how to express that which has already
found a trail down the pink of my cheek.

My name is Ali and I am afraid of being forgotten.

— Ali, age 20

My life is almost as much a mystery to me as it is to others. Sometimes I feel like I'm being pulled in all different directions but I will never find my way because it's never the direction I want to go. I may seem to be an average tall girl with curly hair wearing a light blue Abercrombie t-shirt, but I'm also a human being that has all the potential in the world to grow and love.

But I need to feel safe and protected and necessary. I want to realize what is already there or what I already know but can't see for myself. I want to be a better person... a better me... but still me. I want people to just give us teenagers a chance.

— Tara, age 17

12 | bearing witness

In the rec hall of a small camp in Kent, England, there is a huge sheet of oaktag paper taped onto a cinder-block wall. At the top of the sheet are written three words: "Who Are You?"

Underneath the question, the sixteen year-old campers made a list.

A girl
A little boy in a big world
Beautiful
Wanting to make a huge difference
Hardcore horny
A randomer
The realization of a dream
I don't know

Every single one of us has and inhabits an invisible kingdom. It is the secret life landscaped by
loneliness and neglect. Confusion and chaos. Shame and disregard. It is the emptiness that echoes when the world folds its arms in front of our experiences, leaving us to feel that "no one really knows what it's like." It is the cryptic code etched inside a heart of sorrow that no one else can see.

What is written on the cinder-block walls of our secret worlds? Who haunts the hallways of our hideouts? Most of us rarely speak of our invisible kingdoms. We fear that others will misunderstand, disregard or betray us. We dread confirmation of our worst nightmare: that our highest hurts and deepest dreams truly are unseen.

Melanie from Minnesota illustrates: "My mom says I'll get over him, the guy who took my virginity - that this feeling of rejection will pass. She says that I'll meet someone new. Why can't she see that I don't want this feeling to pass? I don't want to meet someone new. If I can't have my boyfriend, let me at least have my grief."

Ronnie from Texas writes, "I have always felt like an outsider, someone who gets along with people, can think for the whole group, can instigate a program without a glitch, but who has no self-esteem, isn't the right size or shape, whose hair is a little too straight or a bit too puffy. I sometimes stare in the mirror and wonder, 'Who is that?' I look so long and so hard that my face becomes distorted and turns into someone else, either beautiful or absolutely ugly. My mood seems to manifest into my physical being and yet no one ever knows."

And Guy from Manchester, England stutters as he speaks to me through tears, "I can't find the words to say what's in my heart for fear that people won't 'get' me. I can't even find someone to talk to so I can say that I can't even find someone to talk to. How can I put into words how complicated it is to be me?"

The invisible kingdom is the unseen realm that we construct in order to safeguard the inexpressible secrets we keep. It pulses under the surface of our growing personalities, erroneously suggesting that we are seemingly different, oftentimes inferior and ultimately alone in the world. It is the dwelling place of disappointment.

Sixteen year-old Josh from London writes, "I stood on the Tower Bridge, stared deeply into Emma's eyes and for the first time knew that I loved her. But when I looked down, I saw that we were standing on either side of the lift that raises to allow boats to pass beneath. I realized then that we were from two different worlds and this relationship would never last."

Andy in Detroit says, "I have learned that if you push your hurt and pain away and try to forget, it will hit you later in life, but twice as hard. You have to deal with the pain before you can be happy. I have made that mistake in the past by turning to drugs. Sometimes I still do. I know I will have to face it sooner or later."

Orit from Israel told me, "Only after I can endorse my sadness will I be able to find room in my heart for joy again." She dated her soldier boyfriend "for two years, six months and eight days." He was called to appear for service on a Sunday morning but left for Lebanon the night before and was killed crossing the border. "His name was Nitzan, which means 'the bud of a flower.' He will always be inside of me," she said, "but our relationship will never bloom. He is still a part of me but never again will he be a part of the defining moments that make up my life."

I'm an art major in college and I've been having some creative difficulties lately. In the first quarter I was raped. I felt like I needed to be loved so much that I went with some guy back to his dorm room. Maybe I thought that I trusted him. He had been my friend and crush for over a year. Maybe I was sick of being the one that people came to for love advice. I don't know if there is any excuse for my behavior, but my memories are unnerving. Not a day goes by that I don't hear my protests of that time. Does that make sense? I can't forget it. It took me more than a year to get tested for HIV. I went to counseling for four months and improved quite a bit. But my desire and ability to artistically express my feelings and thoughts nearly disappeared. It was much easier to just keep them in. I have come to realize that in order to create and express so that I can understand and be understood, I must deal with my past and present issues despite the pain and fear that may go along with them. I must chip away at the wall I have built around myself and quit hiding from my reality.
– Anonymous, age 21

I went through a very difficult situation when I was younger. I wish that there was someone else that knew what I was feeling on those days when I would trek over to this particular neighbor's house so that he could use me to please himself sexually. I kept going back to his house, week after week, for so long. I kept going back in part because I was twelve or thirteen at the time and didn't understand sexuality and repercussions of action. But more, I think I kept going back because it made me feel special, and that by him wanting my body, I was complete. Always dubbed "the fat boy," it was incredibly gratifying to feel attractive and I guess he played on that need for gratification. Though the time I have spent in therapy has helped me to analyze and make sense of the encounters, I am not yet at the point that I can forgive him. Maybe someday.
–Shane, age 19

The invisible kingdom is the home of our resident ghosts and our indwelling wounds, all laid out upon the back roads of the imperceptible life. Here is where hope is held in safekeeping by an ever enduring silence.

It is the shelter for the solace of sorrow; the welcome mat for the wounds of love; the resting place of loss.

I once had a voice teacher who would unceasingly say, "When you sing, I want to hear what you had for breakfast. Invite me inside. Into your wonder. Into your woundedness. Into all of your realization. And from that place, teach me how to know my own heart."

As I hear my students' stories and collect their emails, I listen for the music inside of them - for the tune in their voices as they tell me of their pain; for the melody of unmerciful memories as yet unsung. And as these resound off the cinder-block walls of their secret worlds, I venture to verify and validate their invisible kingdoms. Though they carry with them the piece of themselves they most want the world not to see, I encourage them to show me. In the words of my friend Aviva, "If you'd like, we can pull up a corner and be sad together."

My friend Eric instructs me that "people just want to be heard. We all want someone to look across the table at us and say, 'I know you' and really mean it. We all feel a little alone in the world, a little disenfranchised from the source where it all originates." It follows then that we must allow people their searching, their mourning, their longing to connect back to that 'once upon a time.'

I remember getting off an airplane, impatiently waiting in line, while the flight attendants bid each passenger a formulaic farewell. "Ba-bye...see ya...come again...watch your step...ba-bye, now." Feeling stressed and a little irritable from the uneasy landing, I frowned at the attendant upon my turn to be greeted. "I see you," said the attendant, smiling compassionately. "I see you and I know."

I remember once attending Yizcor, a Jewish memorial service commemorating all the lives of any loved one that had died. As I settled into my seat on the aisle, the friend next to me asked, "How are you today?" Preparing for the emotionally daunting task before me, I tearfully replied to Tina, "Sad. I'm very, very sad." She looked down at her prayer book and back up at me, then softly said, "Yes." After a few more seconds of silence, she repeated out loud, "Yes." She did not try to deny me, advise me or compare my sorrow to hers. She calmly and kindly gave consideration to my truth.

And I remember a lecture wherein the person in charge sat me down to deliver some last minute instructions. "Now remember," she started, "you can only talk for thirty minutes and you will want to be careful how you word some of your story. Oh, and I just wanted you to know I can see that you have a broken heart." She did not try to fix me, steal it from me or put me back together. She simply and sweetly gave testimony to my lostness.

In the secret lives of teenagers living on the edge of emotion, the healing occurs not just by solving the problem or removing the pain, but by making room for it. It is achieved by creating a sacred and safe space to witness with them their innermost wounds and wonders. In my work with teens, I have learned that healing can be accomplished by receiving their song, saluting their courage and applauding their strength of survival. The mending begins not when we fix for them, but when we reflect back to them, with the universal balm of mercy, what we have witnessed, that they might begin to see their own glory. This is indeed true for anyone, at any age. To learn the message that is hidden we must use the mirror of the heart.

On the day of my twin brother's wedding, I could not understand or explain my sadness to anyone. Then my mother saw me. She sat at the top of a staircase and wept out loud. "You're lonely!" she cried. Her words rolled on a wave of emotion as my secret spilled from her lips. "Oh Scott, I feel how lonely you are and I'm so sad for you." She held my emptiness and cried for me. In Hebrew, the word for mercy is Rachamim and its origin comes from Rechem, which means "womb." My mother wept over my unhappiness; she cried my tears. Carrying my loneliness for me on that day, she enveloped it within the womb of her mercy and I was soothed.

Bearing witness to our secret lives does not extinguish the seeming emptiness. It does, however, soften the starkness of the very emptiness we feel. No human power can ever fully relieve the hole in another's soul. It is not our job to fill their existential void. Our role is to help others find a healthy and more compassionate way of holding and carrying their discomfort within the void.

Emptiness is the scariest feeling because it is the absence of all feelings.
Or maybe it's a combination of every feeling; building and colliding and
exploding - and leaving nothing. So where there should be something left
inside you, it feels like there's just a void. And you want to fill it, but you
have no reserves left. Yet in fact you do! Because emptiness is a reserve in
itself. It's a place to start rebuilding. To step back, take a breath and rethink.
To begin again, the way you want to. Emptiness is the scariest feeling,
but it's the one we all need the most.
– Allison, age 16

Everyone I meet passes through an experiential cycle, from time to time, of rich connection to and deep dislocation from the world. Sometimes we recognize, in moments of blazing beauty, that we are infinitely irreplaceable. Other times we feel, in moments of absolute upheaval, that our entire existence is utterly futile. In our unending search for purpose and meaning in life, we waver. Like a small child who, from the heights of glee, loses his footing and unexpectedly falls down a flight of stairs, eventually we learn that, while sometimes glorious, the world can also be a dangerous place. It is here, in the middle of our disconsolate nights, when we are brought low, that we become acquainted with feelings of true vulnerability. From this place we are utterly exposed to the experience of total abandonment.

Who stands beside us in these seemingly unbridgeable moments?

Who will believe with us in our ability to transcend the darkness and begin again? Who understands, what one teen poetically coins, "my private midnight?"

Carved deeply into a wooden desk at a college in the northeast are the words, "My life sucks." When a teenager tells me a statement like that, I ask him to consider and cherish his present pain. "Let's go outside and look at the full moon tonight," I respond. "Then tell me what you see. Tell me what you are thinking. Tell me what it feels like to be you on the inside. And I will stand beside you and listen." If we can mercifully bear witness to another's internal occupants, he will begin to see, in the midst of the emptiness, his own valor and magnificence. By gently confirming some of the anguish, the other can safely encounter, beyond the darkness, her reflection. By holding with them the heaviness of heartache, they can grasp the meaning of the words, "I am received. I exist. I am enough."

To bear witness is to read the pages in the Book of Days, amidst the discomfort, with courage and compassion. Becca from New Hampshire, challenged me thus: "I'm a loser. That's all I'll ever be." When I disagreed and said, "No you're not," she helped me to see that I was denying her reality. "Then okay," I said. "While I don't see you as a loser, I will accept the fact that you think of yourself that way."

To bear witness is to become the white of the canvas of another person's inner life that is as yet unpainted by suspicion and doubt. Brooke from Long Island explains, "I'm sorry this email is so random. I don't really know why I'm telling you all of this or writing you in the first place, but I guess it's because,

I want to be seen in a certain way."

To bear witness is to stand beside another in the abandon, finding something loving inside of them when they cannot find it themselves. It is to embody the promise they wish to keep in a life riddled with angst, contradiction and desire. It is to be their secret eyes, allowing them to step back, take a breath and rethink, so that they can begin again.

The wisdom we can offer is our unassailable attendance. Our enduring presence. Our never-ending nearness. It is not in the answer to a question or the telling of a story or even the ability to comprehend the issues others are trying to convey. It is the sitting. The walking. The sharing of the time given, allowing them to find their own soul's voice. As one teen instructs:

We come to you because we recognize you as one who can understand.
You share your pain with us, as well as the pain of all the others whose
stories you tell. We come to you for more sharing, recognizing you as someone
who feels like we do: ashamed and uncertain, and sometimes broken.
Somewhere within us is the knowledge that in understanding our pain and
grief, you also understand our need for compassion and friendship. And if
you understand these things, then you must feel them too. In a sense,
we know that you need us just as much as we need you.

In the words of Ali, a Pakistani teenager working the midnight shift as a desk clerk in a London hotel, "Sometimes people get so self-involved. No one really talks to each other. You never know that each person has information we need, that can change our lives. You never know until you shake their hand and talk to them."

In the poetic words of fifteen year-old Alma, who wears earrings in the shape of roses, "Look outside. See that tree, how the wind is beating up on it? Even though the branches are shaking, notice how strongly the leaves hang on."

Joel from Allentown, with adolescent judiciousness, keeps telling me, "I feel ya. I really feel ya."

And Simon in England writes, "I find that it is in these times, when I risk it all for love, that I am at my happiest."

In their letters and emails my students teach us that "there's no such thing as a perfect life; everybody's got something they have to learn to live with." But they also express that they are "moving mountains, many stones at a time." They direct us to our own imaginary castles, deliver us into the hands of hope, and challenge us to a life of joy.

On this long steep road to lifelong happiness, I wish you
comfort in your heart
serenity on your mind
acceptance of your body
courage to embrace the unknown
peace
and a lifetime of friends knocking on the door to your invisible kingdom.

May you always be witnessed and validated, received and remembered.

Live
Because you can

Scott Fried is a health educator and motivational speaker. Since learning of his HIV status in 1987 he has lectured across the United States as well as many other countries, reaching more than a million teens, young adults, the developmentally disabled, parents, teachers and professionals. He was seen on the television daytime drama *Guiding Light* portraying Bart, a young man living with AIDS and is featured in the books *The Faces of AIDS: Lives at the Epicenter, Living Proof: Courage in the Face of AIDS* and *Celebrate Healing: A Time to Heal.* He has been interviewed on numerous television news and talk shows and received the Honorary Star of the Rainbow Award for his work with youth. He is the author of *If I Grow Up: Talking with Teens About AIDS, Love and Staying Alive,* and also produced a musical CD, *As I Grow,* performing eleven songs of hope, gratitude and the resiliency of the human spirit. Scott lives in New York City.

If I Grow Up: Talking with Teens About AIDS, Love and Staying Alive

Musical CD
As I Grow